FE

CHROMATICISM
Theory and Practice

CHROMATICISM
Theory and Practice

HOWARD BOATWRIGHT
Professor of Music Emeritus
Syracuse University

WALNUT GROVE PRESS
Fayetteville, New York

Distributed by
SYRACUSE UNIVERSITY PRESS
Syracuse, New York

Text and musical examples designed by David Ross,
Syracuse, New York, using a Macintosh Quadra 800.

PRINTED IN THE UNITED STATES OF AMERICA
by
Bookcrafters, Inc., Chelsea, Michigan

Library of Congress Catalog Card Number: 94-61072

ISBN: 0–8156–8118–6

Contents

Preface   ix

PART ONE
THEORY

Chapter 1. Derivation of the Tones   3
    INTRODUCTION   3
    THE MONOCHORD   4
    SCALES AND MODES: PENTATONIC TO DIATONIC   8
    DERIVATION OF THE CHROMATIC TONES   14
    SUMMARY OF THE CHROMATIC GROUPS   18

Chapter 2. Tuning   25
    THE PYTHAGOREAN AND SYNTONIC (DIDYMIAN) COMMAS   25
    PYTHAGOREAN TUNING   28
    JUST (NATURAL) TUNING   29
    MEANTONE TUNING   31
    EQUAL TUNING   36
    EQUAL TEMPERAMENT (KEYBOARD)   37
    TUNING BY BEATS   38
    THE PARTIAL SERIES   42
    JUST INTONATION AS AN IDEAL   44

Chapter 3. Intervals   54
    MELODIC AND HARMONIC INTERVALS   54
    MELODIC INTERVALS: THE SPATIAL SERIES   55
    HARMONIC INTERVALS: THE BLENDING SERIES   56
    DIFFERENCE TONES   62
    INTERVAL ROOTS   64
    HEARING AND PERCEPTION   66
    TONALITY   73

Chapter 4. Sonorities   82

DEFINITION OF SONORITY 82

CLASSIFICATION OF SONORITIES: SYMBOLS 84

ROOTS OF SONORITIES 93

FUNCTIONAL ANALYSIS 96

BUILDING SONORITIES 105

Chapter 5. Chromatic Modes   108

THE PARTIAL SERIES VS. THE CIRCLE OF FIFTHS 108

SYMMETRICAL ORDERING OF THE TWELVE TONES 110

CHROMATIC MODES (UNMIXED) 114

CHROMATIC MODES (MIXED) 117

REDUCTIONS OF TWELVE-TONE ROWS 118

PART TWO
PRACTICE

Introduction   129
Chapter 6. Tone-sets   133

DEFINITIONS 133

USE OF THE MATRIX IN MELODIC CONSTRUCTION 136

GENERATION OF TONE-SETS FROM TRICHORDS 141

ANALYSIS OF TONE-SETS 145

Chapter 7. Two-Part Polyphony   147

INTRODUCTION 147

THE TREATMENT OF INTERVALS 149

CANTUS FIRMUS 150

THE COMPLEMENTARY VOICE 152

EXAMPLES 153

Chapter 8. Three-Part Polyphony   155

THE THIRD VOICE 155

CONTRAPUNTAL RELATIONS 156

DISSONANCE LEVEL 157

NOTATION PROBLEMS   159
EXAMPLES   160

Chapter 9. Four-Part Polyphony   164
THE FOURTH VOICE   164
EXAMPLES   165

Chapter 10. The Dissonant Style   170
EXAMPLES   172

Chapter 11. Polyphony With More or Less Than Note-
Against-Note   174
EXAMPLES   176

PART THREE
EXAMPLES FROM COMPOSITIONS

EXAMPLE 145. EXCERPT FROM *STRING QUARTET NO. 2*, FIRST
MOVEMENT   181
EXAMPLE 146. EXCERPT FROM SYMPHONY, THIRD MOVEMENT   184
EXAMPLE 147. EXCERPT FROM THE SONG, NO. 5 OF THE CYCLE, *FROM
JOY TO FIRE* (URSULA VAUGHAN WILLIAMS)   188
EXAMPLE 148. EXCERPT FROM THE SONG, NO. 1 OF THE CYCLE, *FIVE
SONGS* (VICTORIA HILL)   189
EXAMPLE 149. EXCERPT FROM THE SONG, NO. 1 OF THE CYCLE, *FIVE
SONGS* (VICTORIA HILL)   191
EXAMPLE 150. EXCERPT FROM THE SONG, NO. 1 OF THE CYCLE, *FROM
JOY TO FIRE* (URSULA VAUGHAN WILLIAMS)   192
EXAMPLE 152. EXCERPT FROM *HYMNE*, NO. 3 OF *THREE FRENCH
SONGS*   195
EXAMPLE 153. EXCERPT FROM THE SONG, NO. 1 OF THE CYCLE, *SIX
SONGS OF KIERKEGAARD*   196
EXAMPLE 154. EXCERPT FROM *SYMPHONY*, SECOND MOVEMENT   198
EXAMPLE 155. EXCERPT FROM *STRING QUARTET NO. 2*, THIRD
MOVEMENT   202
EXAMPLE 156, EXCERPT FROM *SYMPHONY*, THIRD MOVEMENT   204

EXAMPLE 157. EXPOSITION OF THE FIRST THEME, FIRST MOVEMENT, *SONATA FOR CLARINET AND PIANO*   208

EXAMPLE 158. ENTIRE FIRST MOVEMENT, *STRING QUARTET No. 2*   213

Some Special Cases 242

EXAMPLE 159. EXCERPT FROM *VARIATIONS ON "MIT FRIED UND FREUD ICH FAR DAHIN,"* FOR ORGAN   243

EXAMPLE 160. EXCERPT FROM *"HEUT' TRIUMPHIERET GOTTES SOHN" CHORALE IN TENOR,* FOR ORGAN   245

EXAMPLE 161. EXCERPT FROM *VARIATIONS FOR PIANO*   248

EXAMPLE 162. EXCERPT FROM *LAMENT OF MARY STUART,* FOR SOPRANO, HARPSICHORD AND CELLO (GAMBA)   250

The compositions from which examples have been taken in Part III are published by Walnut Grove Press, Fayetteville, New York. The *String Quartet No. 2* has been recorded by the Manhattan String Quartet on CRI, No. SD, 514-B.

Notes 255

Bibliography 267

Index 271

Preface

THIS IS A BOOK ON MUSIC THEORY, divided according to an ancient pattern into two parts: a theoretical part, being a summary of the writer's view of the musical material from his particular standpoint; and a practical part, which applies these theoretical principles in specific situations—in this case, examples to test certain principles and excerpts from compositions to illustrate their use in actual music.

The pattern, of course, is familiar: it is that of Zarlino's *Le Istitutione harmoniche* (1588), Books I and II being the theoretical part, and Books III and IV the practical part. By Zarlino's time, this pattern was already traditional for treatises on music, and it continued on into the eighteenth century with Rameau's *Traité de l'harmonie* (1722). After Rameau, when equal temperament seemed to promise the solution of many theoretical problems, the emphasis turned to the practical techniques of harmony. Pure theory was dealt with by scientists (Sauveur, Helmholtz), and no longer occupied a major part of music theory books.

In the twentieth century, Paul Hindemith returned to the old pattern. His *Unterweisung im Tonsatz* was announced by its publishers on the dust cover as a work following the great tradition of Zarlino and Rameau. It began with a first volume called *Theoretischer Teil* (1937), and continued with the practical part, Book II, *Übungsbuch für den Zweistimmigen Satz* (1939, and Book III, *Der Dreistimmigen Satz* (1970, posthumous).

Knowing Hindemith's interest in and knowledge of the history of theory, there is no doubt that he was emulating his great Italian and French predecessors, as well as J. J. Fux, whose *Gradus ad Parnassum* (1725) gave him the model for his practical part. Hindemith's vision as a theorist was wider than that of the post-Rameau theorists who turned out harmony book after harmony book all through the nineteenth century and into the twentieth century. Even so, pragmatic need during the years he taught at Yale caused him to write a short book on traditional harmony (1943), about which he said in his preface, "I am consciously taking this step backwards in full realization of its relative unimportance." (Ironically, it has been his most successful book, with translations into many languages, including Hebrew and Japanese).

Hindemith had his moment in mid-career (approximately 1937) when he forcefully expressed his own solution, both in his writing and in his compositions, to the problem of a music no longer dominated by the major and minor keys and traditional harmony.

During the 1940s, the teaching of his theoretical formulations and his pedagogical method (begun with the two-part writing book) had moved far ahead of their realization in his published writing. This was perhaps because he had interrupted his work on the third volume of the *Craft* to produce not only *Traditional Harmony* (1943) and *Traditional Harmony II, Exercises for Advanced Students* (1948), but also *Elementary Training for Musicians* (1946). Some chapters of the three-part writing book were used in mimeograph form by his Yale students after 1945. The book was finally brought to publishable form, though some projected parts were never finished, by three of his former students at Zurich University (Andres Briner, D. Daniel Meier, and

Alfred Rubelli). By the time it appeared in 1970 (seven years after his death), Hindemith's moment as a theorist had passed. Up to this time, an English translation has not yet appeared.

In my days of enthusiasm about Hindemith's theoretical ideas, my colleague at Yale, Quincy Porter, cast cold water on my fire by saying he thought Hindemith would be remembered for his music more than for his theories. At the time, I attributed this view to Porter's being allergic to all music theory, but in retrospect I have to admit that his view was probably correct, if only because art always takes precedence over theory.

When Hindemith left Yale permanently in 1953 to live in Switzerland and to teach at Zurich University (until 1955), I inherited his Yale course called "Basic Principles of Theory," in which theoretical ideas stemming from Book I of the *Craft* were discussed. In one of my last talks with Hindemith before he left for Switzerland, I asked him if I should retain the course format as it was, and he said I should feel free to develop it in any way I wished. During the next ten years, I expanded his treatment of the history of tuning and temperament (with the help of Barbour's book, which had just become available), began to introduce some ideas about chromaticism as an independent system in itself with some influence from Yasser's *A Theory of Evolving Tonality* (1932), which I first saw around 1946 when one of my classmates wrote a paper on it under Hindemith's direction; and I continued to develop Hindemith's theories of chord classification, chord roots, and series expressing tonal relationships and interval values.

The theoretical part of this book, as anyone familiar with the *Craft* will recognize, owes much to Hindemith. But if his word were gospel (as many of us believed it was), some of the formulations as I have given them here are heretical. So, indeed, is the mere idea of a totally chromatic music, which, in its serial form, was castigated in several of Hindemith's major writings (the *Craft,* the introduction to the 1948 version of *Das Marienleben,* and *A Composer's World,* 1952). In the latter work he states that, "A tonal system that cannot be used for *a cappella* singing [by which he means chromaticism] is bound to die sooner or later of anemia" (p. 91). But so will a system which accepts such a limitation; that medium has, in fact, long ago reached its limits, though its beauty is unquestioned.

In the older treatises, the "practical part" takes its illustrations from one of two sources: from examples of previously composed music by composers other than the writer (Zarlino takes many of his examples from Willaert); or from illustrations prepared especially for the work by the writer, or the writer's own compositions. Rameau uses only examples composed by himself, a practice followed by most post-Rameau harmony books, including Hindemith's *Traditional Harmony. Craft* II and III contain only Hindemith's material except for folk songs and one Gregorian plainsong used as a basis for settings. In *Craft* I, however, he includes some examples with analyses from vastly different styles and periods (Gregorian chant, Machaut, Bach, Wagner, Stravinsky, Schoenberg, and Hindemith) intended to support the universal applicability of his theoretical concepts. What the examples make clear is that the theoretical principles are best demonstrated in the examples by Bach, Wagner, and Hindemith himself; therefore the method of analysis was by no means universally appropriate.

Having lived through the experience of Hindemith's attempt to establish a universally applicable system, and having seen Schenker's methods applied to styles ranging from early medieval polyphony to twentieth century music (both of which Schenker himself considered outside the proper frame of music), I take the position that the most appropriate form of analysis is one that relates directly to the composer's method (theory) of working (composition).

For the examples of Part Two, I have chosen the Rameau path, in that I have supplied musical examples of my own, to which the theoretical formulations are directly related.

It is not my concern here to point out how much these formulations may or may not apply to the work of other composers, or how much the music may or may not resemble other music. Since no one has a patent on chromaticism (though Schoenberg fought for priority in the "invention" of twelve-tone serial technique), there must be resemblances between all chromatic music, just as there must be resemblances between pieces in the major mode by different composers.

I should point out, however, that the formulated approach to chromaticism shown here was not "invented" as a theoretical abstraction for which I then wrote some music. It evolved, in fact, from music I had written from 1966 to about 1976, when the procedures were fully formed. Writing about it systematically took place only after 1988, when I decided to put on paper some things that even the most curious analyst (if there should be one) would have great difficulty in ferreting out. It would be an enormous waste of time for anyone to search for tone-rows, or the Golden Mean; or to use set theory (as for atonal music) or to make Schenker reductions; or to analyze harmonic fluctuation or to search for roots or tonal functions.

There is nothing mysterious about how these works were made, and I am willing to take the consequences of having destroyed any possible mystique they may have had by stating clearly what the constructive methods were. What the compositions *are* is a musical question above and beyond theoretical analysis.

A reasonable question at this point would be to ask why anyone should take the trouble to formulate in words things that are clear enough (to discerning ears and eyes) in the music itself. Two of this century's great masters, Bartok and

Stravinsky, left us music without words to explain how it was made. But it is not possible that these composers, whose intentions are so clearly realized in each of the stylistic phases they went through, did not have clear guidelines which regulated what emerged from their minds into musical notation. Such guidelines, always changing, are the substance of music theory—more so than the structural bones taken from that substance in later analysis. But Bartok and Stravinsky apparently did not take pleasure in verbalizing their constructive processes. Bartok devoted an enormous amount of his time to folk song research. Stravinsky was highly verbal about esthetic matters, if someone were there to help him bring his verbalizations to the printed page.

Schoenberg and Hindemith, on the other hand, enjoyed theorizing and verbalizing. Both left large amounts of material to reveal how they thought and worked—not only esthetic cogitation, but specific technical details meaningful to other composers. Both of them, however, warn us against overemphasis on technical details, and remind us that music, as art, cannot be created from such details alone.

Hindemith: "But no one will be so stupid as to assume that what has been impossible throughout all ages is now possible: to create a work of art without creative impulse, simply by burrowing and calculating." (*Craft* I, p. 101).

Schoenberg: "You have dug out the series of my string quartet [No. 4] correctly. . . . That must have been a very great effort, and I do not think I should have mustered the patience for it . . It might be stimulating to a composer who is not yet well trained in the use of series—a clue to procedure, a mere craftsman's reference to the possibility of creating from series. But the esthetic qualities do not open up from this. . . . I cannot warn enough against overvaluing these analyses. . . ." (Letter to Kolisch, *Briefe,* p. 178; quoted in Austin, p. 104).

This book exists because I am one of those composers who does enjoy theorizing and verbalizing. My hope is that these pages will pass on some of the lore of the subject in clarified form, and that they will offer some additional insights into perennial problems.

Howard Boatwright
November 9, 1991
Fayetteville, N. Y.

Part One

Theory

1

Derivation of the Tones

INTRODUCTION

THERE ARE MANY ASPECTS to the history of music—to name a few, the early stages and growth of new forms and various styles, and the invention and exploitation of new instruments, with resulting effects on form and style. These musical aspects are interrelated, and they are also affected by forces beyond music itself, such as economics, sociology and politics.

Along with the above aspects that make music a reflection of man's life and culture, there is another aspect for which there is no history, because it was present before music in human terms existed, and will exist when no such music remains. It is similar to mathematics,[1] in that it existed before mankind began to understand it, and it will be there when and if mankind no longer exists.

The aspect of music to which I refer is the nature of tone and the relationships between tones. The comparison to mathematics is apt, because any relationship can be expressed in mathematical terms. But there can be no history of mathematics—only a history of our on-going grasp of the principles.[2]

Because on this basic level of music we deal only with such

universal concepts as number and proportion, there can be no fundamental differences between basic theories in different parts of the world. The differences will be only in the pace of discovery, not in the fundamental concepts. Perhaps a good analogy could be found in the progress of mankind from the stage of stone tool-making through the Bronze Age. The pace of this progression may vary in different parts of the world, but the stages show the same basic pattern because they follow a line of resistance-to-be-overcome which is implicit in the nature of the materials.

Sophisticated theories about musical sounds and numerical proportions, including cosmological speculations as to their relation to the universe, were known in China before 1000 B.C.[3] Similar theories were developed in Greece by the time of the legendary Pythagoras (after 600 B.C.).

Since no evidence has been able to prove direct transfer of musical-theoretical ideas between the two cultures mentioned above, it would appear that they may have arrived independently at an understanding of concepts that were, in any case, universal.

Of course, we speak here only of basic theoretical concepts. The development of musical art in each region has a character of its own which is a reflection of its culture; the only thing universal about culture is its infinite variability.

THE MONOCHORD

The basic insight shared by more than one branch of humankind was that there is a direct relation between musical intervals and numerical proportions. Each culture has its own legends about the discovery; the Western legend is that Pythagoras noticed it in watching a blacksmith striking an anvil with hammers of different weights.[4] The proportion of the weights to each other gave the musical intervals of the octave (1:2), the fifth (2:3), the fourth (3:4) and a whole-tone (8:9). Pythagoras is said to have demonstrated this principle to himself by hanging a string from a nail in the wall to which he attached different weights. The principle could be demonstrated in other ways: by strings or pipes of different lengths, or by measured holes in pipes.

The commonest theoretical tool—developed in Greek theory and used throughout the Middle Ages for demonstration, learning unknown melodies, and tuning keyboard instruments—was the *monochord*, a single stretched string mounted on a resonating box.[5] Measurements could be marked off along the board under the string. When stopped at the marked points, pitches of the calculated scale could be sounded.

The methods for calculating pitches on the monochord relied at first on the proportions of the simplest intervals: octave, fifth, and fourth, along with the major second, which is the difference between the fifth and fourth. Here follows a brief description of the kind of procedure used.

If a monochord is marked at the middle of the whole length of the string, and stopped at that point, permitting only ½ of the string to vibrate, the pitch sounded would be the octave above the fundamental (1:2).

Example I

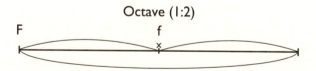

Octave (1:2)

If the whole string were divided into three parts, and stopped at a point permitting ⅔ of the string to vibrate, the tone sounded would be that of the fifth above the fundamental (2:3).[6]

Example 2

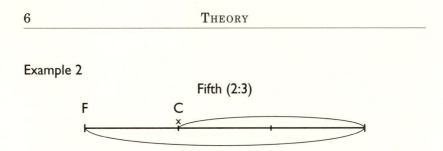

Fifth (2:3)

If the position of this fifth were taken as a starting point, and a similar division into three parts were made from there to the right end of the string, a point marking ⅔ of this new measurement would give the note a fifth above the original fifth.

Example 3

Fifth (2:3)

F   C   g

In tones, the above operation would be:

Example 4

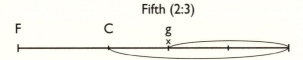

If a measurement is taken from the new tone, *g*, to the right end of the string, (l. to r.), and this length is used in the reverse direction (r. to l.), a tone an octave below the *g* will be found.

Example 5

F   G   g

Descending fourths instead of ascending fifths may also be used to derive new tones. For example, take the point marking the fifth above the fundamental *(C)*. Measure from there to the left end of the string in four parts. Stop the string allowing three of the four parts to sound. This tone *(G)* will be will be a fourth below the starting point *(C)*.

Example 6

Fourth (3:4)

F G ⟵——— C

In practical monochord calculations, instead of using fifths and fourths, the major second (8:9), which is the difference between them, may be used. For example, divide the string into nine parts. Stop the string at the point permitting eight of the nine parts to vibrate. The tone produced *(G)* will be a whole-tone (8:9) above the fundamental *(F)*.

Example 7

M2 (8:9)

F G

The method of deriving new tones from successive fifths will produce a five-note scale after two more operations.

Example 8

Tone derivations   Scale

SCALES AND MODES: PENTATONIC TO DIATONIC

The above scale is called *pentatonic* because it has five tones. However, it is not the number of tones that accounts for its character. Any five notes selected from the twelve pitches do not make a pentatonic scale unless they share the same interval relationships as the example above.[7] These relationships are the result of the method of generation by perfect fifths, carried out four times. Among these relationships there are no half-steps, major sevenths or tritones.

The scale shown above has a particular arrangement of small *(M2)* and large *(m3)* steps. Beginning on *F*, the arrangement is *S S L S*. Starting on other tones, it is: *(G) S L S L, (A) L S L S, (C) S L S S, (D) L S S L.*

These patterns are the *modes* of pentatonic music. The number of modes equals the number of tones in a system.

Example 9

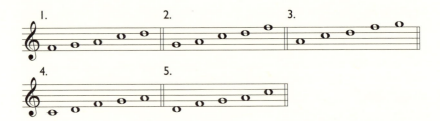

Pentatonic melodies are found in music all over the world. A question we can raise but never answer definitely is whether folk melodies of this type were self-generated among uneducated folk who knew nothing of scales and theory; or whether the performances of educated musicians impressed the ears of the folk, who absorbed the musical language and used it for their own purposes.

Perhaps the truth lies on both sides. The folk singer who follows a good musical instinct would be guided into paths of least resistance by the nature of the musical material—the same paths discovered by the theorist in other ways.

There is also the question of the influence of instrumental sounds on hearing and musical thought. Even the earliest instruments must have provided some models for the aural comprehension of players and listeners. Instruments, as we have seen, must be constructed with some regard for acoustical realities, which in turn leads us back to theory.

However, we do not have to reconstruct a prehistoric situation to illustrate the truth that instruments can produce previously unheard sounds which then may enter the consciousness and become normalized. This situation has occurred in the past two centuries with the development of the equal-tempered pianoforte with sustaining pedals, which has made possible a kind of music previously unimaginable. Can one guess what Mozart might have thought of Debussy's piano music? But by now, these sounds are a familiar language. Still more recently, electronic music has introduced concepts of range and tone color never before available. Electronic composers have said that those new sounds also affected forever the way they composed for non-electronic media.

Since the problem of whether theory or practice comes first cannot be answered definitely because they interact, we shall have to be content in this discussion with the over-simplifications of theory, while acknowledging the enormous complexities of practice. To continue the process of building by means of added fifths, we add a sixth tone to the system. This tone brings in an interval not occurring in the pentatonic system: the *m2 (M7)*.

Example 10

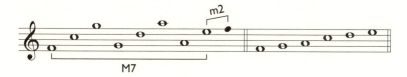

A scale of this kind is called *hexatonic*. There are six hexatonic modes.

Example 11

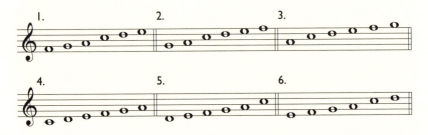

No. 4 above is of particular interest because it is stepwise without a gap. This is the form known in the Middle Ages as the *ut-re-mi–fa–sol–la* hexachord of Guido d'Arezzo on which solmization is based.[8]

The hexachordal scale also occupies a special position among musical formulations because it is exactly one half of the total chromatic material. Its complement is another similarly shaped hexachord at the interval of a tritone.

Example 12

The next stage in adding fifths introduces another half-step and a *tritone* (three successive whole-tones) into the system. This is a *heptatonic* scale, more commonly called *diatonic*, from the designation it had in the Greek system that was the predecessor of our Western scales.

Example 13

There are seven heptatonic or diatonic modes. They can be described as two interlocked four-note groups (*tetrachords*). These tetrachords have only four basic shapes, according to the kinds of steps that lie between the notes. In one case, there are three whole-tones (tritone), and in the others, two whole-tones and one half-tone, with the position of the half-tone varying. Described in this way, the diatonic (heptatonic) patterns are:

Example 14

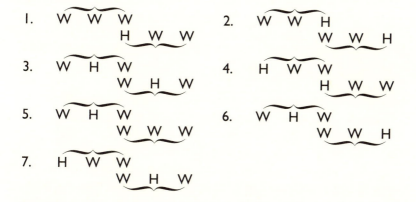

In tones, with one note added at the top to complete the octave, the diatonic scales are:

Example 15

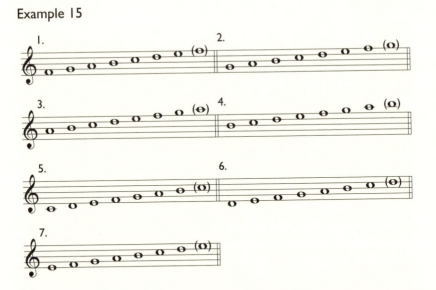

The basic diatonic material has been used selectively in many different cultures and periods. In Western culture, Gregorian chant used diatonic modes, at first designating them by corrupted Greek names for the numbers, one to four—*Protus, Deuterus, Tritus, Tetrardus*. The numbers identified the principal tone of a melody and its ending note, or *final*. Of these, only four were acknowledged: *D, E, F,* and *G* (Nos. 6, 7, 1, and 2 in the above example).

In the Gregorian system (with a precedent in the Greek system), each mode was recognized in two forms: one in which the melody ranged mostly above the final (*authentic*), and the other in which it was both above and below the final (*plagal*). Though there were only four finals, the addition of the plagal forms made an eight mode system. These eight modes were numbered in Latin, alternating authentic and plagal as *Primus* (authentic on *D*), *Secundus* (plagal on *D*), *Tertius* (authentic on *E*), *Quartus* (plagal on *E*), etc. The use of numbers, either Roman or Arabic, is now preferred in discussing the modes of Gregorian chant.

Ancient Greek modes had names deriving from tribes or provinces—Dorian, Phrygian, Lydian, Mixolydian. These names, known to medieval writers through Boethius, were applied to the modes of chant in the eleventh century (Hermannus Contractus, 1013–1054)[9], but they were never officially accepted for liturgical chant, which even today uses numbers. However, the system of modes as developed for polyphonic music did adopt the Greek names, and added two more finals, *A* and *C,* calling them Aeolian and Ionian.

Six finals with authentic and plagal forms made a twelve mode system, expounded notably in a sixteenth century treatise called *Dodecachordon* (Glareanus, 1547).[10]

Of the seven permutations of the heptatonic tones, one (No. 4 of the chart above) never found practical use because its fifth tone was not a perfect fifth above the starting tone.

Diatonic modes, like their pentatonic ancestors, are widely disseminated in folk and art music. Though pentatonic scales were primary in China, heptatonic forms were also known. In India, the scale forms on which ragas are based include (along with non-diatonic patterns) all of the six usable diatonic patterns of Western modality.

The addition of the seventh tone, which produced the diatonic scales, had momentous consequences if judged by its impact on music. We have observed that the five-tone level, free of all close dissonant relationships and the tritone, became a major stopping point for many musical cultures. The seven-tone level has proved to be another such threshold; any move beyond it also has momentous consequences, previously more or less avoided, but now fully upon us in the twentieth century.

In retrospect, we can see that the seventh tone broke through the dividing line between the two halves of the twelve-note tone supply. It added the first of the six complementary tones to the original hexachord.

The new note brings the first tritone relationship into the system. That it was a stranger among the other tones was recognized early in the medieval period when a flattened form of the note was introduced to avoid the tritone, *F–b*. In order to hide this compromise, the *b♮* and *b♭* were not to be used in the same melody.[11] The fact that this substitution created another tritone (*b♭–E*), and that no matter how many times the tritone is hidden, it re-appears in another place, led the theologically oriented medieval writers to compare the tritone to the devil *(diabolus in musica).*

The tritone, in violating the pentatonic-hexatonic limits, adds an element of imbalance and tension that has been the source of much energy in the diatonic system. When diatonic harmony developed—bringing the tritone to the fore in chords, creating tension and resolving it—it made for more forceful situations than are possible in the beautifully balanced pentatonic-hexatonic.[12] The tritone, as the one negative element in the diatonic system, acts in the manner of a catalyst in a chemical reaction; in its presence, everything begins to move.

DERIVATION OF THE CHROMATIC TONES

If we continue to derive tones by adding fifths, the eighth tone carries us over the diatonic threshold onto a new level that is more drastically different from diatonic than diatonic is from pentatonic.

This new level is called chromatic. The term (as with *diatonic,* descended from Greek theory) is most often thought of as related to the division of the whole-tone into half-steps. However, successive half-steps are only one manifestation of chromaticism. A more inclusive definition (though it is negatively expressed) would be: any combination of three or more tones that cannot be expressed within the diatonic gamut (the pattern of the white keys). A simple test would be to try to play the pattern in any transposition on the white keys alone; if a black key is required, the grouping is chromatic, and belongs to that level which lies beyond diatonic.[13]

Let us derive the *eighth tone*, and examine the consequences of this addition to the intervallic relationships of the system.

Example 16

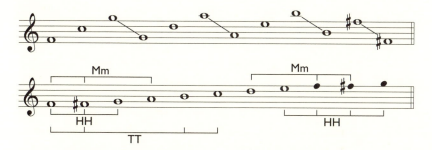

Immediately evident is the combination of two consecutive half-steps, an event which cannot occur in diatonicism (symbol: *HH*).

Then, the *F♯* brings in another tritone *(F♯–C)* together with the original tritone, *F–B* (symbol: *TT*). The diatonic scale can have only one tritone (of course, not counting inversions as different).

Another new conformation occurs in that the *F♯* places a minor third between the tones of the major third, *F–A*. Such a juxtaposition of both major and minor thirds with another tone above or below cannot occur in diatonicism (symbol: *Mm*). The same formula occurs also as *D–F–F♯*.

Above *E, F, F♯* and *G* produce a still larger half-step group (the same symbol, *HH*, is used even though more than two half-steps occur).

The above symbols, *HH, TT,* and *Mm,* indicate three of what we shall call *chromatic formulas.* It is the presence of one or more of these formulas which gives our definition of chromaticism. Their presence means that the diatonic level has been exceeded, and that the interval structure is now on the chromatic level. The over-simplified identification of chromaticism with the twelve tones of the chromatic scale is clearly inadequate, since as few as three notes in certain groupings can indicate chromaticism, just as one dominant seventh chord can clearly indicate a diatonic key.

The addition of the *ninth tone* brings still more chromaticism into the system:

Example 17

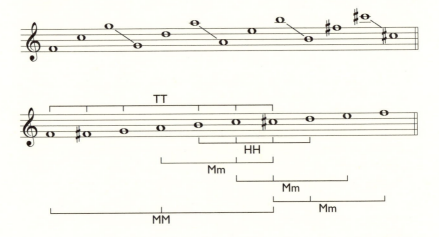

Besides adding another tritone *(C♯–G)*, another pair of half-steps, and three more *Mm* formulas, the *C♯* brings in a new chromatic formula; above *F* and *A* it adds another major third, *A–C♯*, making two superimposed major thirds, another grouping not possible in diatonicism (symbol: *MM*).

The *C♯* also makes a progression of four whole-tones possible: *F–G–A–B–C♯*. This grouping, in itself, is not a basic formula, since it contains the already identified formula, *TT*.

The addition of the *tenth tone, G♯*, increases the chromaticism quantitatively but not qualitatively, since all of the definitive formulas of chromaticism are already present.

Example 18

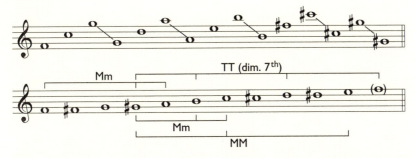

The *G♯ (A♭* adds a minor third to the major thirds, *F–A, G–B,* of the original diatonic scale; and another *MM* formula. It also produces the chord of superimposed minor thirds *(F–G♯–B–D)* which contains two tritones *(TT)*, traditionally called the diminished seventh chord.

The *eleventh tone, D♯ (E♭)* goes one step further towards the total chromatic, but adds no new formula.

Example 19

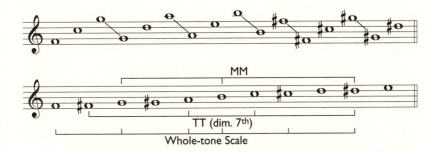

The *D♯* gives another *MM* formula *(D–B–D♯)*, two more Mm formulas, and another diminished seventh chord *(F♯–A–C–D♯)*. It also completes a whole-tone scale *(F–G–A–B–C♯–D♯)*.

The operation that adds the final fifth gives the *twelfth tone, A♯ (B♭)*.

Example 20

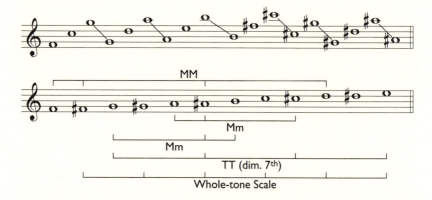

One more *MM* formula is given *(F♯–A♯–D)*, which is the fourth one; two more Mm formulas, and another diminished seventh chord is formed *(G–A♯–C♯–E)*, which is the third one.

A second whole-tone scale is formed: *F♯–G♯–A♯–C–D–E)*, complementary to the one formed after addition of the eleventh tone.

SUMMARY OF THE CHROMATIC GROUPS

The gradual increase in complexity that begins with the addition of the seventh tone is summarized in the statements and diagrams below.

The *Seventh Tone* introduces a group of three successive whole-tones, and the first tritone (ultimately there are six).

The *Eighth Tone* brings in the second tritone and the first two *Mm* groups (ultimately there are twelve).

The *Ninth Tone* brings in the third tritone, a group of four whole-tones, two more Mm groups, and the first augmented triad (MM, ultimately there are four).

The *Tenth Tone* introduces the fourth tritone, four *Mm* groups, the second augmented triad, and the first diminished seventh chord (ultimately there are three).

The *Eleventh Tone* brings in the fifth tritone, five whole-tones (Whole-tone Scale 1), two *Mm* groups, the third augmented triad, and the second diminished seventh chord.

The *Twelfth Tone* brings in the sixth tritone, Whole-tone Scale 2, two *Mm* groups, the fourth augmented triad, and the third diminished seventh chord.

(See Example 21, next page)

The diminished seventh chords shown above are only one form resulting from the combination of two tritones *(TT)*. There are five basic combinations shown in the chart below, in which the tritones are separated by a half-tone, whole-tone, minor third (these are the diminished seventh chords), major third, and an augmented third (fourth).

The combinations a half-tone or an augmented third apart (1 and 5) are similar in that both contain two tritones and two minor seconds or major sevenths. These are among the harshest possible sonorities; they have no place in traditional harmony, but frequently appear in dissonant chromatic music.

The combinations a whole-tone or a major third apart (2 and 4) are also similar to each other, in that they are sonorities which can be produced within the whole-tone scale, and are only mildly dissonant.

The combinations a minor third apart (3) are unique in that they contain only tritones and minor thirds, and do not change shape when inverted. The ambiguities of this structure (the diminished seventh) have been exhaustively explored in nineteenth century harmony.

Example 21

Example 22

Combinations of Two Tritones (TT)

1. Half-tone	2. Whole-tone	3. Minor 3rd	4. Major 3rd	5. Aug. 3rd (4th)
1 - 2	1 - 3	1 - 4	1 - 5	1 - 6
2 - 3	2 - 4	2 - 5	2 - 6	2 - 1
3 - 4	3 - 5	3 - 6	3 - 1	3 - 2
4 - 5	4 - 6	4 - 1	4 - 2	4 - 3
5 - 6	5 - 1	5 - 2	5 - 3	5 - 4
6 - 1	6 - 2	6 - 3	6 - 4	6 - 5

The three-notes combinations with both major and minor thirds above or below a given note *(Mm),* one of the distinguishing characteristics of chromaticism, also occur in harmonic form in which the half-step is expressed as a major seventh or a diminished octave *g* (a. below).

Example 23

The form which treats the half-step as a minor ninth or augmented octave is very much harsher than the one in which it is a major seventh or diminished octave (b. below).

Example 24

Though there are twelve occurrences of the *Mm* formula within the chromatic octave, there are basically only four shapes, excluding those that are spaced wider than a ninth. These are (enharmonically spelled):

a: m6–m3,   m3–m6
b: M6–M3,   M3–M6

The above groupings are found in I^7 and III^7 chords in minor keys (darkened notes in the example below).

Example 25

It can be seen from the chromatic groupings given in several of the examples above that the principal combinations already exist within the constraints of so-called traditional harmony, since that system includes the minor scales, and in its advanced stages, permits alteration of the chords formed from the major and minor scales.

Here is the melodic minor scale, showing some of the chromatic formulas within it:

Example 26

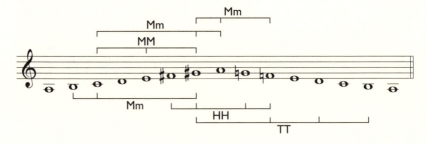

The harmonic minor has a very conspicuous *Mm,* usually avoided melodically, but all the formulas are present.

Example 27

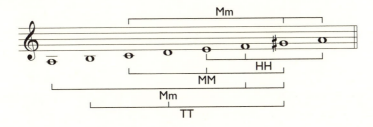

The major scale, of course, has no chromatic formulas, but the alteration of certain scale steps can bring them in (I refer here to those that include a chromatic formula, but not to those that are only chromatic respellings of basically diatonic groupings). Some of these alterations are:

1. Lowering or raising the second step (fifth of the V^7):

Example 28

TT (Combination 4)   MM (Whole-tone)

2. Raising the fifth of a major triad:

Example 29

MM

3. Changing any seventh chord to a diminished seventh:

Example 30

The above account of the derivation of the twelve pitches within the octave, and a survey of some possible combinations of those pitches, should make it understandable that from the time the $b\flat$ became an optional note in the tenth century through the development of the full chromatic keyboard in the Renaissance, utilization of the chromatic material was to present an irresistible challenge to composers. Before that utilization could occur, however, many problems concerning the pitch relations of these twelve notes had to be solved. At this time, it is only too easy to say, "Why bring up pitch relations and tuning problems now that we have equal temperament?"

The first objection to this attitude is that we have equal temperament only on keyboard instruments, and even there its appropriateness for early music is challenged. For the vast majority of musicians—singers, string players, even wind instrument players—there is no such thing as equal temperament. Equal temperament for keyboard instruments and as a means of establishing approximate norms for chromatic music is a hard-won gift—one that should not be accepted without understanding how and why it was acquired. To accept it blindly is to risk only a superficial understanding of the forces which underlie the realities of interval, scale, melody and harmony, whether diatonic (tonal) or chromatic (non-tonal).

2
Tuning

THE PYTHAGOREAN AND SYNTONIC COMMAS

IN THE PREVIOUS CHAPTER we have used a method of scale building that relied on superimposed fifths. In actuality, such a process, using true fifths of 2:3, cannot be carried out in *tuning* a scale, as any amateur who has tried to tune his own piano will testify. We shall examine here some of the tuning problems which were overcome after centuries of experience, leaving us apparently free nowadays to move around in chromatic space like astronauts inside a space ship.

The method of scale derivation used above is called *Pythagorean* because Pythagoras and his followers used similar methods, though in their case only to reach seven pitches within the octave. In Pythagorean tuning, some serious problems are encountered even at the diatonic level.

One problem is that the main tuning intervals—fifth, fourth and major second—cannot be strung out in sequence without starting a spiral that never returns to a pitch an exact octave (or its multiple) away from the starting point.

If the derivation of the twelve chromatic tones shown here were realized in true pitches using fifths of 2:3, the thirteenth note which comes after *A♯ (B♭)* ought to be *F,* seven octaves above the starting point. But it would be found that it is a small interval above that, the proportion of which is 524288:531441. This interval, equal to about a quarter of a half-tone, is called the *Pythagorean comma* in the West because Pythagorean theorists first calculated it; Chinese theorists knew it even earlier.

The fifth is not the only interval by which to demonstrate the phenomenon of the Pythagorean comma; it occurs in any superimposition of the basic intervals. Twelve superimposed fourths fall short by a Pythagorean comma; six whole tones of 8:9 exceed the octave by a Pythagorean comma.

The following diagram illustrates the Pythagorean comma by comparing the octave above *F* with the tone arrived at by six calculations of 8:9.

Example 31

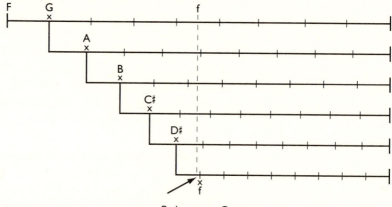

Pythagorean Comma

It is not only in circles (or spirals) intending to arrive back at the starting point that problems appear. Early in diatonic scale formation another important discrepancy shows up.

At the fourth step in the superimposition of fifths (*F–C–G–D–A)*, the *A* forms a major third with *F,* but this tone was perceived even in Greek times as "too high," in spite of the perfection of the method by which it was derived.

Greek theorists were divided into two factions over this issue. One followed Pythagoras, who insisted that what was provable mathematically must be correct; and the other followed Aristoxenus, who said that for the student of musical science, sense perception was a fundamental requirement.[1]

The Pythagoreans formed the interval of a major third by superimposing two whole-tones of 8:9. Mathematically, the result was the same as adding together four intervals of 2:3.

$$8:9 \times 8:9 = 64:81$$
$$2:3 \times 2:3 \times 2:3 \times 2:3 = 64:81$$

In the second century A.D., the astronomer and mathematician, Ptolemy, gave a number of tables of various diatonic tunings.[2] These included one of his own and one by Didymus, a late Greek theorist, which showed a major third formed from the combination of the whole-tone 8:9 with the slightly smaller whole-tone, 9:10. The major third formed had the proportion 4:5; it can be formed on a monochord by division into five parts. Mathematically it may be shown as $8:9 \times 9:10 = 72:90$, or 4:5.

The difference between the above third and the Pythagorean third is called the *Didymian* or *syntonic comma;* its ratio is 80:81.

As with the Pythagorean comma, it is approximately a quarter of a half-tone. The difference can be demonstrated on a monochord as follows:

1. Divide the string into nine parts. At the division mark farthest to the left, stop the string permitting eight parts to vibrate. This sounds the whole-tone, 8:9, above the open string.
2. Take the position of the above whole-tone and again divide the string into nine parts. The division mark farthest to the left again gives a whole-tone, 8:9. If the string is tuned to *F,* these two steps will have given *F–G* and *G–A,* $8:9 \times 8:9 = 64:81$, or the

Pythagorean third, *F–A*.

3. To derive the 4:5 third, divide a string of the same length as in 1. above into five parts. The division mark farthest to the left will give the third, 4:5, *F–A*.

4. Compare the positions of the two *A*s. The Pythagorean *A* is noticeably higher (further to the right) than the one formed by the 4:5 division.

Here is a diagram showing the divisions described above.

Example 32

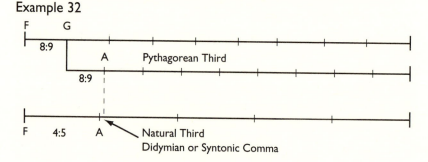

PYTHAGOREAN TUNING

Demonstrations of the tonal system and tuning methods of the Middle Ages (for example, the monochord instructions given by "Odo of Cluny" and Guido d'Arezzo) were Pythagorean, in that they were based on the fifth, fourth and major second, deriving only the Pythagorean third, and not the 4:5 third.

During the period of polyphony in which fifths and fourths were the principal intervals, a tuning based on perfect consonances was entirely satisfactory. Chromatic notes were added to the diatonic *gamut* beginning with alternate forms, *b♮* and *b♭*, to avoid the tritone, *F–b*. Besides alteration to avoid the tritone, notes were gradually added to achieve the half-step progression, *mi–fa*, in various locations because of transposition (mutation). These notes were found on the monochord by extending the Pythagorean method through further steps. By the fifteenth century, complete chromatic monochords were constructed by Pythagorean calculations (Hugo de Reutlingen, 1488).[3]

So far we have discussed interval sizes in terms of proportions. This is how they were understood by ancient theorists. From this point on, we shall change to a more recent way of describing intervals. C. H. Ellis, the translator of Helmholtz's *On the Sensations of Tone* (1878),[4] introduced a method in which the octave is given the value of 1200 *cents,* and each interval assigned a proportionate value. Here are the values of the main Pythagorean intervals in cents:

8	5	4	M2	M3	m3	m2	Pythagorean comma
1200	702	498	204	408	294	90	24

Intervals of the diatonic tunings of Ptolemy and Didymus which differed from Pythagorean tuning were:

M3	M2	m3	m2	Didymian comma
386 (4:5)	182 (9:10)	316 (5:6)	112 (15:16)	22

JUST (NATURAL) TUNING

In the medieval period, the 4:5 third and its contrast to the Pythagorean third aroused little interest. But by the time of the Renaissance, when polyphony had begun to favor imperfect consonances over perfect consonances, and when the full resonance of triads was preferred to the open sound of doubled fifths, theorists began to search for ways to get rid of the sharp Pythagorean third in favor of the more mellow and better blending 4:5 third. The first writer to offer a monochord not completely Pythagorean was Bartolomeus Ramis de Pareja (1482).[5] Here is a list of the major thirds in his monochord. All the major thirds of diatonic (white key) notes are 4:5, 386 cents.

C–E	*386*		*F–A*	*386*
C♯–F	406		F♯–B♭	406
D–F♯	408		*G–B*	*386*
E♭–G	408		A♭–C	408
E–A♭	412			

There were dozens of monochord constructions during this period with varying mixtures of Pythagorean and natural intervals, as we now call them. Any tuning in which natural intervals are predominant over Pythagorean intervals is called *Just intonation.* In all such tunings, however, some intervals, because of the obstinacy of the commas, are not consistent with the others. This problem can be observed even when we apply the principles of Just intonation to the C major scale.

Example 33

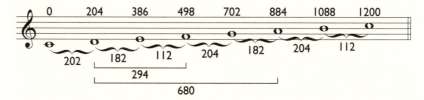

In this tuning, two intervals do not match the others: the Pythagorean *m3, D–F* (294), and the fifth, *D–A* (680) are each flat by a syntonic comma (22 cents). The position of the comma can be changed by rearranging some intervals, but it cannot be eliminated. Extension of this tuning to include all the chromatic tones also extends the comma error to different pitches.

MEANTONE TUNING

A tuning process which retained the desired natural third (4:5) but eliminated the excessively false fifth of the Natural tuning was first accomplished by Pietro Aron in 1523.[6]

Aron's method was to begin with a natural major third tuned so that it was "sonorous and just." He then went through four stages of the circle of fifths: *C–G, G–D, D–A, A–E*—making each one "a little flat." If the flattening were not too much or too little, the *E* arrived at in the fourth operation would match the already established third at the octave. Since the error of the syntonic comma was 22 cents, each of the four flattenings would have been 5.50 cents (¼ comma), if correct.

Example 34

The fifths in this system would be 696.50 cents (702 – 5.50), noticeably but not disturbingly low. A major triad in this tuning would have a sweet and mellow sound because of its just third, considerably more pleasant than the triad with a pure fifth and a Pythagorean third.

The second step of the scale, *D*, formed by the second superimposed fifth would have been flattened by ½ comma, or 11 cents. The whole-tone, *C–D*, would then be 193 cents (204 – 11), or exactly half the size of the natural major third, 386 cents. Hence the term *meantone*—the whole-tone lying in the middle of the major third.

Meantone tuning is carried through a number of additional operations to derive the twelve chromatic pitches. All tunings of this category end up with the usual impasse at some point, in which certain intervals are unsatisfactory. In the tuning of Aron, the trouble is delayed until the tone $G\sharp$, which makes what is called a *Wolf Fourth* with the $E\flat$ below (463 cents, 35 cents too low), and a *Wolf Fifth* with the $e\flat$ above (732 cents, 35 cents too high). This means that keys likely to include these intervals have to be avoided.

Here is Aron's Meantone temperament with the numbers in rounded cents:

Example 35

Meantone Temperament (Aron). Figures in cents (rounded).

C	C♯	D	E♭	E	F	F♯	G	G♯	A	B♭	B	c	c♯	d	e♭
0	76	193	310	386	503	579	697	773	890	1007	1083	1200	1276	1393	1510

Meantone tempered fourth, 5 cents too high.

Meantone tempered fifth, 5 cents too low.

"Wolf" fourth, 463 cents.

Natural major third, 386 cents.

"Wolf" fifth, 737 cents.

Meantone tempered whole-tone, 193 cents.

Zarlino in 1571 arrived at a similar Meantone tuning, but by another method. He used a Euclidian way of finding the mean proportional, or the *geometric mean* between two points.[7]

There are various mathematical and mechanical procedures for finding the geometric mean. One way is as follows:

1. Divide the string into five parts to find the natural third, 4:5.
2. To find the geometric mean between the tones of the major third, *C* and *E:*
   a) Draw a circle with a compass taking the whole length of the string as the diameter.
   b) From *E,* drop a perpendicular line to the point it crosses the circle.
   c) Measure from this point to the right end

of the monochord.

d) Transfer this measurement up to the string. This point is the geometrical mean between *C* and *E,* which is the tone *D* at 193 cents (half of the major third, 386).

Because of the small scale of the operation when done on 8½ by 11 inch paper, factors even as small as the thickness of a pencil line may cause noticeable errors. To check the accuracy of the calculation, find the middle point between *C* and *E;* the geometric mean should be on the right side of this point.

Example 36

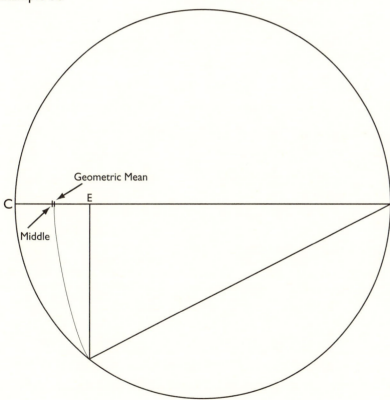

Geometric division is one of the two possible ways of finding an intervening pitch between two established pitches. The other way, already carried out above, is *arithmetic division:* simply dividing the space on the line in two equal parts. Whereas geometric division gives unequal lengths along the string but equal sizes in cents, arithmetic division gives equal lengths along the string but unequal sizes in cents. To illustrate, geometric division of the octave (1200 cents) would give two tritones of 600 cents: *C–F#* and *F#–c.* Arithmetic division would give a fourth (498) and a fifth (702). The following diagram shows the two divisions:

Example 37

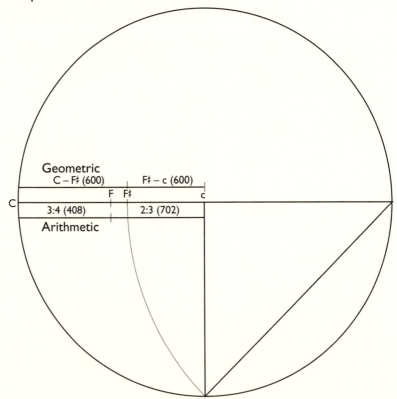

Note that in arithmetical division, the interval on the left

is smaller in pitch size than the one on the right. The string
length between *C* and *F* is a smaller proportion of the distance from *C* to the right end of the string (¼ of the length)
than *F–c*, which is ⅓ of the distance between *F* and the right
end of the string; therefore *C–F* is a smaller interval than
F–c, though on the ruler, they measure the same.

This division is called *arithmetic* because the two intervals
formed fit into the arithmetical series, 1, 2, 3, 4, 5, etc. In this
series each number has one digit higher or lower than its
neighbor to the left or right. All of the proportions we have
dealt with so far have been parts of this series: 1:2, 2:3, 4:5,
8:9. As shown in the diagram above, when an interval of this
kind is divided arithmetically on the monochord, two smaller
intervals are formed, the smaller one on the left. If arithmetic
division is shown in figures, the proportion should be placed in
superparticular form (larger number first, or on top) in order
for the sixes to appear in the same sequence as they appear on
the string, left to right.

The procedure for finding the two intervals produced by
arithmetic division is:

1. Place the interval in superparticular form, higher
   number over lower.
2. Multiply the upper number by 2.
3. Add the lower number to the upper. This is the
   smaller interval.
4. At the right of the smaller interval, place a proportion in which both numbers are one digit less that
   those of the first proportion. This is the larger interval.

The following diagram will illustrate the above procedure:

Example 38

$$\frac{2 \times 2}{1 + 2} = \frac{4}{3} \qquad \frac{3}{2}$$

Octave   Fourth   Fifth

EQUAL TUNING

The goal of most renaissance tuning theorists was to achieve the natural sweetness of pure thirds, and to hide the comma errors in the least conspicuous way, which was achieved best by some type of Meantone tuning. As it became more necessary to be able to perform the same mode or scale on different starting points within the chromatic *gamut,*[8] there was less emphasis on the beauty of pure thirds and more on obtaining freedom of movement within the twelve tones. The "Wolf" intervals of Meantone tuning obviously stood in the way of such freedom. The goal then shifted, necessarily, towards equalization of the intervals to make movement through the chromatic *gamut* possible in all directions. If equality of interval sizes were to be the goal, then each interval would have to sacrifice some of its purity for the good of them all.

Keyboard instruments were not the only ones that needed an even division between the twelve tones; instruments with frets, such as lutes, guitars, and viols, needed to divide the fingerboard into twelve proportionately spaced stopping points (frets).

There were numerous proposals for mathematical and mechanical means of accomplishing this task, but it was Vincenzo Galilei (1581)[9] who found a practical and effective way of achieving a satisfactory result. Galilei observed that the smaller of the two half-tones formed by arithmetical division of the 9:8 whole-tone, 18:17 (99 cents), was closest to the correct size for twelve even half-tones in the octave.

Example 39

$$\text{Arithmetic Division of 9:8}$$
$$\frac{9}{8} \times \frac{2}{9} = \frac{18}{17} \quad \frac{17}{16}$$

Using 17:18 (103 cents) would produce too few frets in the

octave, and 19:18 (93 cents), too many. Therefore, Galilei set
the frets by successive measurements of 18:17 (99 cents).
This division, however, still left a correction to be made at
the octave, since twelve 18:17 half-tones would be half a
Pythagorean comma short of the octave (1188 cents).

Numerous suggestions were made as to how this correction could be achieved, some involving complex mathematical calculations. In the end, the most practical way was to set
the frets, then change the position of the bridge, slightly
shortening the string length. All the established proportions
of 18:17 would then be changed to another proportion ap-
proximating 200:212 (100 cents), the *equal tempered half-
tone*. Verification of the amount of string shortening required
would be accomplished by sounding the pitch of the harmonic in the middle of the string; if it agreed perfectly with
the tone sounded by the fret position of the octave, the ad-
justment would be correct.

EQUAL TEMPERAMENT (KEYBOARD)

Practical tuning was achieved on fretted instruments earlier
than on keyboard instruments. Since viols and plucked
instruments were principally used for melody, they were
more tolerant of the sharp thirds of equal temperament than
keyboard instruments, especially the organ, on which
sustained sound made the sharpness of the thirds more un-
pleasant. According to Nicolo Vicentino (1555),[10] fretted
instruments were always in equal temperament,
but Meantone tuning was common to all keyboard instruments. It is not insignificant that Meantone tuning, with its
natural thirds, survived more than a century after the general availability of equal temperament; nor that now there is
a revival of interest in this tuning for music written prior to
the nineteenth century. Besides the better-sounding triads,
it is felt that Meantone tuning heightens the coloration of
different keys through its very inequality—a feature wiped

out by equal temperament.

Attempts to solve tuning problems led sixteenth and seventeenth century theorists in two directions.

One direction was to experiment with further division of the octave by means of split keys or multiple keyboards, seeking to retain the best possible thirds and to mollify the "Wolf" intervals. Both 19 and 31 keys to the octave offered good possibilities, but 24, 25, 29, and others had their advocates.

The other direction was to carry on with a twelve-note system, but to seek more exact division by mechanical or mathematical means expressible in figures and applicable to a monochord. Calculations were made to establish the proportional figures for twelve half-tones assuming a very large number for the fundamental and half that number for the octave above. Such measurements were given for the figures 10,000–5,000 (one of the commonest), 100,000–50,000, and 200,000–100,000. Not known in Europe until a French publication in 1789 was a calculation of equal temperament by the Chinese, Prince Chu Tsai-yü in 1585[11] using a scale of 1,000,000,000–5,000,000,000 (for example, C = 1,000,000,000, $C\sharp$ = 943,874,312, D = 890,898,718, etc.).

TUNING BY BEATS

Among the many mathematicians who made calculations such as the above was Marin Mersenne, whose great work, *Harmonie universelle* (1636–37),[12] included all that was known in tuning theory at that time. Along with geometrical and mathematical solutions for forming equal tempered monochords, he offered a crucial suggestion to the practical tuner: "The fifth beats once in each second when it is tempered as it should be."

By the time Mersenne made this suggestion, tuning "by ear" had already had a long history which included Aron (1523), who said that fifths should be "a little flat," and Giovanni Maria Lanfranco (1533), who said that fifths should be tuned so flat "that the ear is not well pleased with them," and the thirds as sharp as can be endured.[13] The enlargement of the major third, in particular, suggests that this tuning by ear led to an approximation of equal temperament.

The importance of Mersenne's suggestion was that it supplied something definite to go on, not merely such vague phrases as "a little flat," or "as sharp as can be endured."

The term, "beat," as used by Mersenne, requires some comment. It shows recognition of a phenomenon not examined scientifically until considerably later, principally by Helmholtz (1872–78).[14] The phenomenon is that when two vibration frequencies occur together, a third frequency is created which is the difference between them. To illustrate, when two frequencies are shown together in wave form, their curves fall together at a point which is the multiple of the two frequencies. Below is a diagram with small numbers, two and three. These waves fall together on the first of every six units.

Example 40

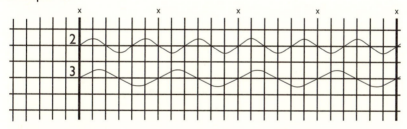

The coincidence of the two waves results in a increase of loudness at that point. When these reinforcements occur at speeds slower than about twelve–fifteen per second, they are perceived as throbbings or *beats*. At more rapid speeds they are no longer perceived separately, but merge into low-pitched sounds called *difference tones*.[15]

This cross-over speed is a perceptive threshold, and corresponds to that at which a series of separate images is perceived as a moving picture.

The reality of difference tones was observed by Giuseppe Tartini (1754),[16] who called them *terzi suoni,* and taught his students to listen for them in finding correct intonation for intervals (double-stops). Helmholtz studied them with the use of special resonators to make them more audible.

Pitches and beats are both expressed in vibrations per second. If A is 440 vibrations per second and another pitch sounding with it is 439 vibrations per second, the difference is one vibration per second. The point where the waves coincide is at 193,160 vibrations; this will occur once each second when the strings are vibrating at 440 and 439.

We speak in this case of a mistuned unison that beats once each second; but Mersenne's hint concerns fifths. Here again, Mersenne's perception was correct, but far ahead of the scientific explanation of it. The beating heard in a mistuned fifth is not between the fundamental pitches (which do produce a perceptible low difference tone), but between higher partials (overtones) that should form a unison, but do not unless the fifth is in perfect 3:2 proportion. The following example illustrates:

Example 41

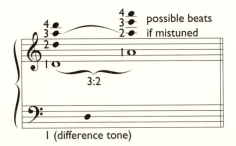

It can be seen that the third partial of D is, theoretically, the same frequency as the second partial of A: 880 vibrations. Very slight flattening of A could cause its second partial to be 879, which would produce beats of one per second.

What Mersenne indicated was that this amount of flattening for each of twelve fifths would distribute the 24 cents Pythagorean comma throughout the circle at 2 cents per fifth. The resulting tempered fifths would be, in Ellis' terms, 700 cents each.

Of course, once the idea of counting fifths became a part of the tuner's technique, intervals other than fifths could be tempered if the necessary number of beats per second were determined. Further, similar intervals, such as a pair of thirds, could be tempered exactly alike if the speed of the beats were matched.

In 1706, a famous tuning contest took place at Jena in Germany between Johann George Neidhardt, who had just published a book on *Beste und leichteste Temperatur der Monochordi,* and Johann Nicholaus Bach, a cousin of Johann Sebastian.[17] Neidhardt was prepared with a monochord measured with figures accurate to six places. J. N. Bach tuned by ear, which must have meant that he counted beats. Bach was judged the winner because a singer found it easier to sing a chorale in $B\flat$ minor with his tuning. Barbour summarized the situation between the tuners who measure and those who listen when he writes:

> Unfortunately, the more mathematically minded writers on equal temperament have given the impression that extreme accuracy in figures is the all-important thing in equal temperament ... But they needed a Mersenne to tell them that the complicated tables could well have had half their digits chopped off before using, and that, after all, a person who tunes accurately by beats gets results that the ear cannot distinguish from the successive powers of the twelfth root of 2.[18]

THE PARTIAL SERIES

The problems of tuning have led us at this point to including the mention of two fundamental acoustical phenomena which were not recognized during the centuries that the various systems of tuning were developed. The phenomena are partial tones (the Partial Series), and difference tones, which cannot be understood without reference to partials. These phenomena are to play an important part in the next chapter, which deals with intervals. Therefore, this is the place to show how partials merged into the mainstream of tuning and interval theory.

Though the connection between string lengths, proportions, and intervals had been common knowledge since Greek times and fully explored on the monochord, the notions that a single fundamental tone produced by a string could at the same time contain the pitches of the intervals formed by the division of that string, and that the relative strengths of these partial vibrations were related to the quality or *timbre* of the tone were not clearly perceived and stated by anyone prior to Mersenne. In *Harmonie universelle,* he refers to two problems posed by Aristotle (384–322 B.C.) as a basis for his own discussion headed, "To determine why a vibrating string gives several sounds simultaneously." Aristotle's questions were: "Why does the low note contain the sound of the high note?" (Problem 8); and "Why is it that the octave, the concord of the upper note, exists in the lower, but not vice versa?"

Mersenne says, "It must be remarked that the struck string gives at least five different sounds simultaneously, of which the first is the natural sound of the string, serving as fundamental of the others ... Now these sounds follow the ratio of the numbers, 1, 2, 3, 4, 5." He identifies these pitches as 1, fundamental; 2, octave; 3, twelfth; 4, double octave; 5, double octave plus a major third. Also, he says, "The sound of each string is all the more harmonious as it causes to be heard a great number of different sounds simultaneously."[19] This statement, according to Wood, is the first clear association of quality *(timbre)* with partial tones.

J. B. Fourier (1768–1830) and G. S. Ohm (1787–1854) added important mathematical data to develop the theory of tone quality analysis, but the principal systematic explanations were by Helmholtz. The first mechanical device for converting tones into analyzable wave forms was the Phonodeik by the American physicist, D. C. Miller (1916).[20]

The Partial Series is generated according to the progression cited by Mersenne, and mentioned before in connection with arithmetic division. This means that the vibration number of each partial is: the frequency of the partial multiplied by the series number of the partial.

The fundamental *C* below the bass clef, 64 vibrations per second, is often used for a model series. The *A,* lowest space on the bass clef, 110 vibrations, can also be appropriately used, since its fourth partial is 440, the standard pitch at this time in the United States.

For calculations involving proportions but not specific pitches, series numbers are less clumsy than vibration numbers. Here is a chart for reference, showing the Partial Series on *A*, 110 vibrations, up to the seventeenth partial, which is as high as regular notation can be used to represent partials. Intervals, proportions, and sizes in cents are included in the chart.[21]

Example 42

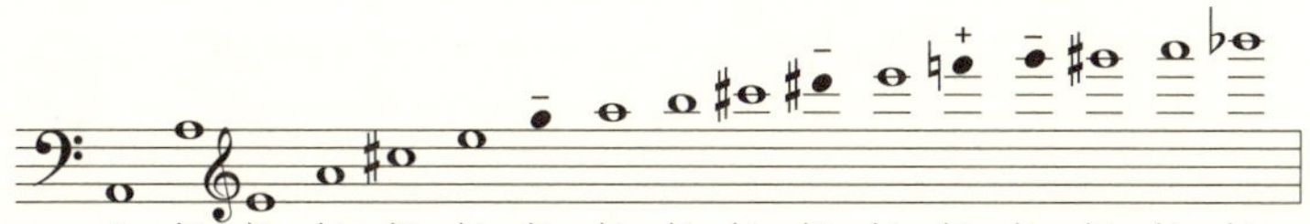

String divisions	1	½	⅓	¼	⅕	⅙	⅐	⅛	⅑	¹⁄₁₀	¹⁄₁₁	¹⁄₁₂	¹⁄₁₃	¹⁄₁₄	¹⁄₁₅	¹⁄₁₆	¹⁄₁₇
Frequencies	110	220	330	440	550	660	770	880	990	1100	1210	1320	1430	1540	1650	1760	1870
Partial numbers	1	2	3	4	5	6	7	8	9	10	11	12	13	14	15	16	17
Intervals	8		5	4	M3	m3	m3–	M2+	M2	M2	M2–	m2+	m2+	M2–	m2+	m2	m2
Proportions	1:2		2:3	3:4	4:5	5:6	6:7	7:8	8:9	9:10	10:11	11:12	12:13	13:14	14:15	15:16	16:17
Sizes in *cents*	1200		702	498	386	316	267	231	204	182	165	150	139	128	120	112	106

Partials can be calculated by intervals directly in musical notation, not using vibration numbers, pitches in cents, or proportions. The ability to erect the series of intervals over any tone is a basic skill. Also, one must know which interval lies between which partial numbers. Previous calculations with proportions can be helpful in developing this skill, because the proportion numbers of an interval *are* its partial numbers. Fluency with the Partial Series is necessary for the calculation of difference tones, since they are most easily determined by the difference between partial numbers rather than vibration numbers. Also, the consonance and dissonance of intervals has to be examined according to the coincidences or clashes between the partials of each tone in the interval.

JUST INTONATION AS AN IDEAL

The idea of "Just intonation" (i. e., including the natural third), first shown in the tunings of Ptolemy and Didymus in late antiquity, was neglected in the Middle Ages in favor of Pythagorean tuning, but emerged when Bartolomeus Ramis de Pareja (1482)[22] introduced four natural thirds into his monochord. Ramis and other theorists of the time were attempting to achieve better sounding triads through the so-called Meantone tuning. Attention was also being given to the problem of using more distant keys, and an equal temperament was being sought, first for fretted instruments and then for keyboard instruments. At the same time, Just intonation remained a philosophical and mathematical problem that interested some of the greatest minds of the period—not only musicians but astronomers and mathematicians, among them Johannes Kepler (*Harmonices mundi,* 1614) and Marin Mersenne. Both of these men worked out monochords not merely to find an acceptable tuning for combinations of intervals sounding together, but to find the ideal pitch for each tone in relation to the generating tone (that given by the undivided string). For Kepler, the astronomer, this problem involved imageries in which the mathematics of musical intervals were compared to the mathematics of the planetary system.

A system which placed all the tones in ideal order was approached by Kepler in two of his monochords, and by Mersenne in several of his spinet and lute tunings. However, all of these tunings involved one or more Pythagorean or other odd intervals with complex proportions. For example, Kepler has a *G♯* (over the fundamental, *C*) which is at 794, 2 cents (called *Schisma*) larger than the Pythagorean *m6* of 792, 81:128. Also, he has a Pythagorean *A (M6)* of 906, 16:27, and a *m7* of 1018, 5:9, inversion of the small *M2*, 9:10. Mersenne has a tuning which uses a *D* of 182 (9:10) leaving a large half-step of 134 (a comma larger than 112, 15:16) between *D* and *E♭*, as well as a *B♭* of 1018 (inversion of 9:10).[23]

The requirements for the ideal arrangement of pitches would be:

Example 43

Intervals	Proportions	Cents
5 and 4	2:3 and 3:4	702 and 498
M3 and m3	4:5 and 5:6	386 and 316
M6 and m6	3:5 and 5:8	884 and 814
M2, difference between 2:3 and 3:4	8:9	204
M7, inversion of 8:9	9:16	996
M2, difference between 3:4 and 4:5	15:16	112
M7, inversion of 15:16	8:15	1088

All of these tones can be achieved on a monochord by the use of intervals with simple proportions—using them directly, taking the difference between them, or adding them together. Curiously enough, of the nearly two dozen historical Just intonations given by Barbour, the only one meeting the above requirements is by a relatively unknown Scotch theorist, Alexander Malcolm (Edinburgh, 1791) whose monochord was included in Rousseau's dictionary (1798).[24]

The following diagram shows the twelve chromatic pitches ideally tuned to the generator.

Note that there are three sizes of half-steps if the notes are read consecutively, with a variance between the largest and smallest of 42 cents *(Minor diesis)*. The largest half-step (15:16, 112) is the difference between the major third and the fourth. This half-step occurs where the natural system involves a letter change: *C–D♭, D–E♭, E–F, F♯–G, G–A♭, B–C.* In each of these cases, the half-step 112 goes together with a smaller one of 92 cents *(major chroma)* to form an 8:9 whole-step of 204. In places where the natural system calls for the small whole-step of 9:10, 182—i. e., between *D–E* and *G–A*— the half-step of 70 cents *(minor chroma)* is used: 70 + 112 = 182. The difference between the major and minor chromas mentioned above is the syntonic comma, 22 cents.

Example 44

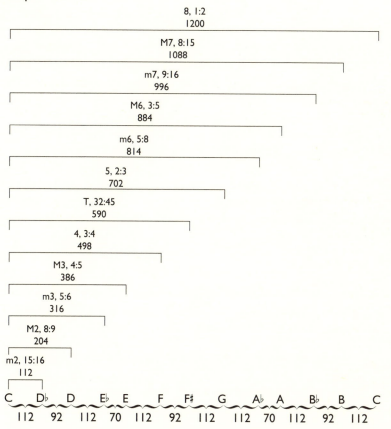

Just intonation had a twentieth century advocate in Paul Hindemith,[25] who erected a chromatic system of that type by a method different from that of the old monochord calculations, but necessarily leading to the same result. Having the Partial Series at his disposal (a phenomenon unknown to early theorists), he used vibration numbers of the partials added together or subtracted from each other to produce the vibration frequencies for all the tones in relation to one generator. The vibration numbers used are only those of partials one through six (the *senario*).

Taking as a fundamental the frequency of *C* below the bass clef at 64 vibrations per second, he uses the first six partials to calculate the other tones, bringing them down or up into the same octave as *C* when necessary by dividing or multiplying. For example, he finds *G* above *C* by taking its third partial (3 x 64 = 192) and dropping it down an octave by dividing it (192 ÷ 2 = 96).

To find *F,* he treats the fourth partial of *C* (4 x 64 = 256) as though it were a third partial, and divides it by 3 (256 ÷ 3 = 85.33), getting the *F* into the same octave as C.

For the next tone, he takes the fifth partial of *C* (5 x 64 = 320) and treats it as a third partial (320 ÷ 3 = 106.550) to get *A.*

Treating the fifth partial of *C* (*e*, 320) as a fourth partial yields *E*, 80 vibrations.

Example 45

The rest of the chromatic notes are found by similar calculations; the pitches arrived at are the same as those in the Malcolm monochord and in the chart above.

Hindemith uses language concerning his chromatic system which echoes Kepler's neo-Pythagorean images. After the first two steps, he writes:

> Anyone who has followed the path which we have taken from *C* through *g* to *G* will have no difficulty in understanding the origin of *our planetary system* (italics mine).

In a later passage, he writes:

If we think of the series of tones grouped

around the parent tone, *C* ... as a *planetary system,* the *C* is the *sun,* surrounded by its descendent tones *as the sun is surrounded by its planets.*[26]

Hindemith's neo-Pythagoreanism, which permeated his theories, came to full fruition in his opera about Kepler, *Die Harmonie der Welt* (first performed in 1957), the title being a translation of *Harmonices mundi.*

In the nineteenth century, just about the time that equal temperament had finally penetrated the conservative bastions of the Meantone-tuned organs of Europe, scientists showed an intense interest in Just intonation with Helmholtz as the leader, and his English translator, A. J. Ellis following closely behind. Helmholtz added as the last three appendices to *On the Sensations of Tone* sections called: XVII, *Plan for Justly-tuned Instruments with a Single Manual;* XVIII, *Just Intonation in Singing;* and XIX, *Plan of Mr. Bosanquet's Manual,* which was an enharmonic organ with fifty-three pitches making possible Just intonation in all keys.

In Appendix XVII, Helmholtz describes his own experimental harmonium with thirty pitches to the octave for all major keys; minor keys needed only twenty-eight pitches. Four valves or pedals set differently for each key could extract the necessary pitches for Just intonation.

Appendix XVIII is a defense of Just intonation in singing, with particular reference to the British system of *Sol–fa* (movable *do*), which Helmholtz heard demonstrated in England and which he greatly admired.

In Germany, with his Justly-tuned harmonium, Helmholtz carried out experiments with singers who were accustomed to accompaniment by an equal-tempered piano. When he omitted the third or sixth, let the singer take it alone, then compared it to the natural, tempered or Pythagorean pitch (any one of which he could produce on his harmonium), he found that the singer had invariably chosen the natural interval. He writes:

> After this experience, I think no doubt can re-
> main, if any doubt existed, that the intervals
> which have been theoretically determined in
> the preceding pages, and there called natural,
> are really natural for uncorrupted ears; that
> moreover the deviations of tempered intona-
> tion are really perceptible and unpleasant to
> uncorrupted ears; and lastly that, notwith-
> standing the delicate distinctions in particular
> intervals, correct singing by natural intervals
> is much easier than singing in tempered into-
> nation.[27]

Apparently Helmholtz's views on natural intonation in the
1872 edition were contested, since he added a defensive
statement to the Fourth Edition (1877):

> I do not doubt for a moment that many of
> these antagonists of mine really perform very
> good music, because their ear forces them to
> play better than would really be the case of
> they had actually carried out the regulations
> of the school, and played in Pythagorean or
> tempered intonation ... When the organ took
> the lead among musical instruments it was not
> yet tempered. And the pianoforte is doubtless
> a very useful instrument for making the ac-
> quaintance of musical literature, or for domes-
> tic amusement, or for accompanying singers.
> But for artistic purposes its importance is not
> such as to require its mechanism to be the ba-
> sis of the whole system of music.[28]

Hindemith, whose chromatic system required twelve tones
within the octave, reflects Helmholtz's view of the piano in
his *Craft* (1937):

One has only to have seen how the most fa-
natical lover of the piano will close his ears in
horror at the falseness of the tempered chords
on his instrument, once he has compared them
a few times with those produced by a
harmonium in pure intonation, to realize that
with the blessing of equal temperament there
entered into the world—lest the bliss of musical mortals be complete—a curse as well: the
curse of too easy achievement of tone-connec-
tions. The tremendous growth of piano music
in the last century is attributable to it, and in
the "atonal" style I see its final fulfillment—
the uncritical idolatry of tempered tuning.[29]

The pursuit of Just intonation on instruments of fixed
pitch was doomed to frustration in Helmholtz's time because
of mechanical difficulties which caused great problems in
playing even fairly simple pieces. With modern electronics
and computer technology, these problems could have been
overcome in the twentieth century.

Perhaps the real problem is that our ears (minds) only too
readily simplify that which is too complex into some less
complex equivalent. Take, for example, the interval $C–D\sharp$, or
$C–E\flat$. Just intonation would tune the notes in relation to a
tonality, while tempered intonation would make both spellings *sound* the same. Our ears, having no context other than
the two pitches, hear them as a minor third, whether they
are exactly 5:6, or a tempered third, 250:297 approximately;
or some other proportion, provided it does not bring the interval too close to a major second or a major third (this is a
range from about 6:7, 267 to 13:16, 359, a span of 92 cents,
the major chroma).

Along with our willingness to accept complex intervals (in
notation) as their simpler equivalents (in sound), we can also
perform the reverse operation: to hear what is simple in no-

tation as something more complex, or even to change our conception of the same pitch in a given context. In the example which follows, the $G\flat$ in the top line emerges from an $E\flat$ minor triad and a diminished seventh chord; but when the G minor triad appears below, it changes its function to that of a leading-tone, $F\sharp$, and resolves to G. Though on the keyboard the pitch cannot change, the new function creates the illusion of a change. Since in the original scoring this note is played by a solo violin, a sensitive player will actually adjust the pitch upwards as soon as the G minor harmony sounds.

Example 46

Chausson, *Poéme*

Academic discussions of exact intonation can lead the practical musician to conclude that there must be no such thing as "in tune." Yet he knows, without scientific analysis, what he *thinks* is in tune, particularly if he is a string or wind instrument player, or a choral conductor.

The reality is that there is no exact order in the realm of pitch, except the one imposed by equal temperament (which is seldom "exact" in practice).

We are able to tolerate one or more kinds of intonation at the same time, if the pitches and tone colors help us to separate the systems. This occurs with string, or wind instruments, or voice in combination with a tempered piano or organ. In an orchestral situation, some soloists deliberately tune their instruments at a pitch level slightly above the orchestra, and some pianists request a slightly higher tuning to avoid sounding "flat" at their first entrance after an opening *tutti*.

String quartet players may have different ideas about melodic intervals (thirds and leading tones), but they tune their open strings in perfect fifths (Pythagorean), and spend hours of rehearsing any conspicuous octave doublings for which there can be no tolerance of falseness; or in adjusting sensitive triadic moments.

Though Barbour can explain why an *a cappella* choral composition performed in Just intonation would end up flat because of commas shifting in the modulations,[30] there are good choral groups who do not lose pitch, even in very difficult music.

What all the above means to the theorist or composer trying to cope with the chromatic world is that he need not worry too much about intonation, though he cannot pretend the problem doesn't exist, even in chromatic music of a relatively conservative kind. Of course, the problem is solved (too easily in Hindemith's view) on pre-tuned, tempered instruments. But other kinds of players or singers have to make constant adjustments on a moment-to-moment, situational basis, and they must do so in spite of the ambiguities of chromatic notation. Ease of reading (i.e., consideration for our diatonic reading habits) ought to be the primary objective in the notation of chromatic music since function shifts so often and so unpredictably. If the situation is totally non-functional, the performer will produce something in the vicinity, let us say, of Gb–$F\sharp$; if anything suggests function, down or up, the player will respond to it (if he has enough time) by pitch inflection. Octaves and fifths, of course, must be in tune or they are intolerable—one of the reasons why these intervals occupy a subordinate place in totally chromatic music.

3

Intervals

MELODIC AND HARMONIC INTERVALS

WE HAVE SEEN that the basic units of music are the proportional relationships of two pitches, called *intervals* because of the space between them, though that space is not their only important characteristic. We shall now examine those intervals which are most usable in a closed musical system: the fifth, fourth, the two thirds, two sixths, the sevenths, seconds and the tritone.

Intervals occur in two dimensions of music: tones in succession (as in melody), or sounded together (as in harmony).

In melody, the spatial aspect of an interval is primary: are the notes close together or far apart? In harmony, the relative blending or clashing of the two sounds is the primary factor; do they form a "sweet blending," or do they appear to disagree with each other.[1]

Our feeling for *tonal space* (high or low, far or near) must be derived from our experience with movement in that space, just as we learn to judge physical space from our experiences within it, a skill cultivated to an extraordinary degree by athletes. It is, of course, through making vocal sounds that we experience the relative effort required for high or low; and by hearing these sounds, we relate the higher frequency tones from a given source to more vocal effort, and low frequency tones to less effort. The player of a wind instrument also has the opportunity to experience the connection between pitch and effort expended. But the player of any instrument producing high and low pitches with little or no physical effort (such as the keyboard instruments) has to grasp this basic aspect only vicariously, as would a person who has never been able to walk or run, but has had to move around by mechanical means.

The shape taken by melodies for different media reflects the conditions of musical space indigenous to the particular medium. Vocal melody, therefore, will not assume the same shape as a typical keyboard melody; violin melody will not be like that particularly suited to the trombone. In the literature, of course, there are many instances of song-like melody for instruments, and the voice is sometimes expected to do things more suited to an instrument than to the voice. Electronically produced melody, a phenomenon of our century, may escape space limitations as easily as the occupants of a space capsule escape gravity.

MELODIC INTERVALS: THE SPATIAL SERIES

It has always been the task of music theory to organize its material in a graded fashion according to criteria which it may set up for special purposes. If we were to grade intervals for melodic use according to the proximity of the pitches to each other, we would have a series of intervals expanding above and below from the unison to the octave, extending the series, if necessary, to the second octave or further.

Example 47

Spatial Series

◄Unison̲m2 M2 m3 M3 4 T 5 m6 M6 m7 M7 Octave

The scale of relative melodic values, shown from left to right, places the two notes a half-step below and above (leading-tones) in the first degree of relationship, The fifth, an extremely important interval in harmonic contexts, is distant from the starting point, and is of lower rank in the melodic hierarchy than the seconds. As hundreds of years of melodic development in chant have taught us, leaps beyond a fifth are beyond the usual limits of vocal melody (how many singers nowadays are likely to miss this interval in sight-reading unless they are firmly supported by a chordal context?).

We can see that intervals at the right end of the series have the least of what the earlier intervals have most: the binding quality of contiguousness. For this reason, the intervals at the right end of the series are favored in the sort of twelve-tone music which wishes to emphasize the individuality of each pitch.[2]

HARMONIC INTERVALS: THE BLENDING SERIES

From the earliest treatises to more recent ones, theorists have placed intervals in order according to the impression they make on the ear when sounded together. Many figures of speech have been used to describe these impressions, but basically they all agree that on the one hand there are intervals which fall easily upon the ear, and on the other hand, those that fall harshly. The most detailed classifications among the old treatises were those of the thirteenth century, of which Franco of Cologne is one. Franco's classification of intervals still reads well; it is based on what he perceives, not only on the relation of concords and discords to numerical proportions, which was so important to more ancient theory. Here is the passage, using modern terminology for the intervals:[3]

By concord we mean two or more sounds so sounded at one time that the ear perceives them to agree with one another. By discord we mean the opposite, namely, two sounds so combined that the ear perceives them to be dissonant. Of concords there are three species: perfect, imperfect, and intermediate.

Concords are perfect when the two sounds are so combined that, because of the consonance, one is scarcely perceived to differ from the other. Of these there are two: unison and octave.

Concords are imperfect when the ear perceives that two sounds differ considerably, yet are not discordant. Of these there are two: major third and minor third.

Concords are intermediate when two sounds are so combined that they produce a concord better than imperfect, yet not better than perfect. Of these, there are two: fifth and fourth. . . .
. . . Of discords there are two species: perfect and imperfect. Discords are perfect when two sounds are so combined that the ear perceives them to disagree with one another. Of these there are four: half-tone, tritone, major seventh and minor sixth.

Discords are imperfect when the ear perceives that the two sounds agree with one another to a certain extent, yet are discordant. Of these there are three: whole-tone, major sixth and minor seventh.

> Observe that both concords and discords can
> be endlessly extended, as in the fifth plus octave
> and fourth plus octave, and similarly by adding
> the double and triple octave, if it be possible for
> the voice.

Though we are hardly able to improve on Franco's percep-
tions, and indeed the usual modern classification is less detailed, we now have more direct means of explaining what we
hear. Modern acoustics shows us the that the Partial Series,
unknown to Franco, is real, not just a set of numbers.

Intervals, of course, are the units of the partial structure, being the combination of any two numbers in the series. Though
among the components of any single tone certain partials may
be present or not present; or strong or weak; or exactly in place
within the harmonic series or distorted to irregular
proportions; for the purposes of interval theory we
may unhesitatingly use the perfect model of the series,
1, 2, 3, 4, 5, 6, etc., in organizing the interval hierarchy. We
shall use the Partial Series to explain the differences between
intervals, assuming for theoretical purposes the presence of all
partials, and setting aside for the moment the function of the
partials in creating timbre or tone color in the individual tones.

The words "sweet blending" are prophetically appropriate,
for the impression of consonance is related to the coincidence
(blending) of the partials from two different fundamentals in
the lower end of the series; and it is the lack of such coincidences in the lower partials and the presence of clashes which
produce the situation in which "the ear perceives them to disagree with one another."

We have already shown in a diagram (Example 41) how the
partials of two tones sounded together, but slightly mistuned,
may produce beats because certain overtones fail to agree exactly at the unison. The interval shown was a perfect fifth. The
point at which the unison was supposed to occur was between
the third partial of the lower tone and the second partial of the

higher tone. These partial numbers are the same as the proportional ratio of the interval sounded: 3:2. From this we deduce the following formula:

> The lowest unison formed between the partials of two simultaneously sounding tones will be at the partial numbers corresponding to the ratio between the tones.

Helmholtz states the above principle, and gives a table and a musical illustration of the intervals, 8, 5, 4, *M6, M3, m3*. This, he says, "is the order of the consonant intervals beginning with those most distinctly characterized, and then proceeding to those which have their limits somewhat blurred ..."[4]

Much of Helmholtz's discussion of the consonance-dissonance question concerns "roughness" caused by beats among the higher partials. Consonance is defined not so much by the presence or absence of coinciding partials as by the disagreeable beating between those that do not coincide. The order of consonance-dissonance is the same by either approach.

The following example gives the intervals with some of their partials written out to show the point of blending. The octave is omitted here because all of its partials are simply duplicated. The blending point of the tritone is not shown because of the uncertainty of its intonation, and because the proportions arrived at in natural tuning involve such high partials (32:45 or 45:64) that they are not notatable.

Example 48

(8)   5   4   M6   M3   m3

Example 48 (continued)

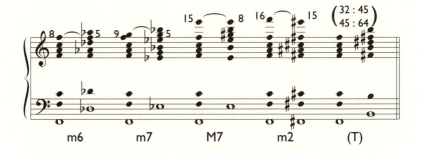

If we wish to make a series which ranks the intervals according to the lowest blending unison, we arrange them in order according to proportion numbers, left to right.

Example 49

Blending Series

Intervals:	8	5	4	M6	M3	m3	m6	m7	M2	M7	m2	T
Proportions:	1:2	2:3	3:4	3:5	4:5	5:6	5:8	5:9	9:8	8:15	15:16	32:45
												45:64
Cents:	1200	702	498	884	386	316	814	996	204	1088	112	590
												610

In effect, the starting point of the series (the octave) is the ultimate blending of two frequencies, and admits no deviation in its tuning. The tritone, at the other end of the series, is shown in two sizes derived from other intervals in natural tuning, but the unison blendings indicated by these numbers are too high up in the series to create any consonance, or to offer any guide in tuning. The intonation of the tritone is as indefinite as the octave is definite. In untempered intonation, its pitches have to be determined by melodic inflection according to context.

While we may regard the octave and the tritone as isolated extreme points, the intervals that fall between these points (5 through *m2*) form an even progression from consonance to dissonance. Division into categories—perfect consonance, imperfect consonance, etc.—are arbitrary, and only reflect the attitude towards degrees of consonance at a given time in music history. Debussy's treatment of dominant-type chords or pentatonic chords without thirds in parallels, and in complete disregard for what had been doctrines about the need for resolution of dissonance to consonance, show that his sensibilities had led him to cross some of those arbitrary barriers. The same is true of Schoenberg with his famous phrase about "the emancipation of dissonance" which sought to remove all barriers to the use of the most complex tone combinations. These changes of attitude, a product of artistic impulses, do nothing to alter the immutable fact that intervals *are* different from each other, and for reasons that have nothing to do with art, but with nature.

If we were to call dissonance consonance and consonance dissonance, and attribute opposite qualities to them in our verbal descriptions, we would not change the fact that a polar relationship exists between the two extremes. The conformation of the Blending Series would not be changed by reading it backwards; we would only change our position from one pole to the other.

If we were to look for some non-subjective dividing line between consonance and dissonance, it may be found in the dividing point between the twelve intervals from octave to tritone. The first six intervals lie within the *senario*.[5] The other six intervals have blending partials (and ratios) which involve numbers above six. The minor sixth could be regarded as the turning point between consonance and dissonance, since it has one number within the *senario* and one number above it (5:8)—this could be an explanation for Franco's purely subjective decision to place the minor sixth among the discords.

In the diagram below, all duplicates at the unison or octave are omitted, leaving only the tones with partial num-

bers below six; they, as well as the blending partials, will
continue to duplicate each other in higher octaves.

It will be observed that all the partials which produce
clashes have odd numbers, in this case, only 3 and 5. New
clashes above the first six partials are produced at 7, 9, 11,
13, 15, 17, etc., having less and less aural impact as they go
higher.

Example 50

DIFFERENCE TONES

In Example 41, which shows how beats are formed, it was
also shown that the interval of a fifth produces a difference
tone; in this case *A* 440 minus *D* 293 gives 147, low *D*.

The phenomenon of the difference tone will occur when
the pitches are accurate within a certain margin; the slight
flattening of the fifth for equal temperament and the presence of beats, for example, does not prevent difference tones
from occurring.

Partial numbers rather than frequencies can be used to
calculate difference tones. Every interval in which the proportion numbers are separated by only one digit will produce
a difference tone which is the frequency of the fundamental.

Example 51

In the cases shown above, the effect of adding the fundamental as difference tone to the sound spectrum of the interval:

a. supports the lower tone of the fifth and major third,
b. supports the upper tone of the fourth; and
c. in the case of the minor third, also adds a pitch not contained in the interval.

A practical consequence of the difference tone phenomenon is that organ builders can make two smaller pipes tuned a fifth apart to produce the difference tone an octave below the bottom pipe instead of building a single long pipe to produce the low pitch directly as a fundamental.

In the case of the fifth, there is only one difference tone (3:2 lies just above 1), but for intervals higher in the series there may be a gap between the lowest partial and the fundamental. With the fourth, a second order difference tone *(dt)* may be formed between the first *dt* and the lowest note of the interval. With the *M3,* a third order *dt* is formed between the first order *dt* and the lowest note of the interval. With the *m3,* a fourth order *dt* is formed between the first *dt* and the lowest note of the interval.

Example 52

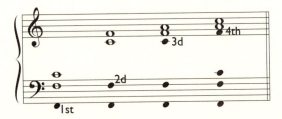

If the partial numbers are more than one digit apart, the first order *dt* is not the fundamental. For example, 5:3 has a first order *dt* of 2; but the second order *dt* is the difference between 3 and 2, which is 1.

The minor sixth, 8:5 has a first *dt* of 3; but the second *dt* is 2, the difference between 5:3; and the third *dt* is 1, the difference between 3:2.

Example 53

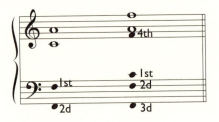

INTERVAL ROOTS

Intervals within the *senario* will produce difference tones doubling or tripling the fundamental at the octave or double octave. For those intervals already containing an octave duplication of the fundamental (2 or 4), these doublings account for the feeling that such intervals have a *root* tone, more conspicuous than the other notes. The fifth and major third have their lower tones supported in this way. The fourth has support for its upper tone, which enhances the impression that it is the inversion of the fifth, The minor sixth (8:5) also has support for its upper tone, causing it to have the effect of an inversion of the major third.

It can be observed in the above examples that the *m3* and the *M6* get no support from their difference tones. These two intervals compared to others of the *senario* are rootless, easily subordinated to the intervals with roots. This is the reason that a *M6* added to a major triad is easily overwhelmed by the root of the triad.

Example 54

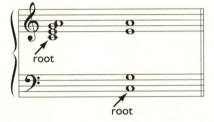

The rootlessness of the *m3* is one reason for the preference in older music for closing with a major triad *(tièrce de Picardie)* rather than a minor triad, even when the mode in use has a minor third.

The minor triad has dissonant conflicts among its difference tones, and the lack of repose in the chord results from the overwhelming competition of other pitches against its lowest tone. By contrast, all difference tones reinforce the root and fifth of a major triad.

Example 55

From what we have seen of the formation of difference
tones for intervals of the *senario,* we can state the principle:

> Difference tones will fill all the space between
> the lowest tone of an interval and the funda-
> mental; also, any space between the main
> notes if they are non-adjacent partials.

While we have numbered the difference tones, 1st, 2nd,
etc., the numbering is only our sequence of calculation; the
formation of difference tones in actuality is simultaneous.

The above principle means that the higher the partial
numbers of an interval, the more "baggage" it must carry be-
neath it in the form of difference tones. A scale of values
based on difference tones alone is simply the order of the proportions in the partial series. The intervals with the simplest
proportions receive the most acoustical support from the difference tones and carry the least amount of baggage; the intervals with the more complex proportions have the least
support and carry the largest amount of baggage.

HEARING AND PERCEPTION

The age of the computer has taught us much about the function of the brain, a super-computer which has evolved with
us in the process of survival. It has astonishing power to
sort, grade, organize and store billions of *bits* of information.
When faced with the information brought to it in the sounding together of two fundamental frequencies with their
overtones and difference tones, it probably reacts first to the
level of stimulation resulting from the excitation of many or
fewer nerve endings in the inner ear, those which are re-
sponsive to given frequencies and carry their electrical
signals to the brain.

After this first reaction to stimulation in the ear, a second
phase occurs which records the sensations in memory. In
this process, it compares the tones to each other and to previ-

ously recorded aural sensations, and grades, classifies, and stores them.

To process all this information, the brain's "program" asks certain questions. The first ones concern the sensory effect. Is the effect of the interval smooth or rough? Is the interval in the high or low pitch range? Other questions concern the ranking of the tones in relation to each other. Does one have a stronger impact than the other? Do they seem equally strong, or is there no clear impression of a difference between them? If one appears to be stronger, is it the lower one or the higher one?

As for the impression of roughness or smoothness, the number of pitch-points excited in the ear by the interval is probably the main factor:

> more pitch-points stimulated = rough sound;
> fewer pitch-points stimulated = smooth sound.

The adjectives smooth and rough, of course, belong to the vocabulary of tactile sensations. It is the nerve endings in our fingers which are stimulated when we rub them over a surface. A rough surface is one which stimulates a great many nerve endings; a smooth surface allows the finger to pass over it with a minimum of individual prickles. The difference between a silk shirt and a hair shirt is another illustration of this principle in the tactile realm. A consonance is "as smooth as silk;" a dissonance is "as scratchy as a hair shirt."

Taste is not the question dealt with in these classifications. There will always be those who take pleasure in the ease and comfort of silk, and those who may feel uplifted by struggling against the discomfort of a hair shirt.

Returning to the ear itself, we may use the well-known illustration which shows the snail-shaped *cochlea* of the inner ear uncoiled.[6] Along its surface are tiny hair fibres *(ciliae)* standing up like algae in the fluid which fills the *cochlea*. These fibres react to movements in the fluid which are caused by the motions of a membrane which lies at one end of the cochlea's chamber. The movements of this membrane are brought to it through a gear system of three tiny bones which carry impulses from another membrane (the *eardrum*) at the end of a small air passage leading to the outer ear. External vibration frequencies enter the outer ear in the form of tiny fluctuations in air pressure caused by the motion of various sound sources, such as vibrating strings, reeds, pipes, drum heads or plates.

However, vibration frequencies from external sources which enter the outer ear do not account for all that we ultimately perceive as sound. The parts of the ear—the air column that leads inward to the eardrum, the small bones between the eardrum and the membrane at the start of the *cochlea,* the fluid in the cochlea, the fibres imbedded in the surface of the cochlea—all of these behave somewhat in the manner of the vibrating parts of an instrument. It is in this way that the ear, receiving a simple, overtoneless, oscillator-produced sound from the exterior may add partials to the sound as it passes through the hearing mechanism *(aural harmonics).* Likewise, on receiving two or more simultaneous pitches in any conformation similar to the partial series, the activated hearing mechanism will respond as a whole, adding the missing partials lying below or between those received. These are the difference tones. Also, partials lying above the received pitches will be formed by adding together the partial numbers of the sounding pitches and of each other; these are called *summation tones.*

Difference tones and summation tones are called collectively *combination tones.* Also, because these sounds (including aural harmonics) may be formed in the ear, they are sometimes called *subjective tones.*

Whether combination tones and summation tones are produced in the ear, outside of it, or both is of no consequence in considering them in relation to music theory. We can hear only a small number of the harmonics which are produced by any rich tone, but the *principle* of the harmonic series has to be considered whether the partials are always audible or not. In distinguishing one interval from another theoretically, difference tones and summation tones may be considered without concern for audibility itself, that factor being immensely variable.

Summation tones, though present in theory, have less practical value than difference tones because they lie in the range above the real sounds which is also inhabited by overtones; whereas difference tones lie below the real sounds without competition in the same pitch range.

Summation tones, as with difference tones, are calculated in successive orders. For example, 5 + 3 forms 8. This summation tone combines with the real tones to produce other summation tones: 8 + 3 = 11, 8 + 5 = 13. The sounding interval 5:3 results in the difference tone, 2. This difference tone with the real tone 3 results in another difference tone, 1 (fundamental). The difference tone 3 combines with the real notes 5 and 3 and the first summation tone to produce more summation tones: 2 + 5 = 7, 2 + 8 = 10, 2 + 10 = 12, 2 + 13 =15. The difference tone 1 combines with 3 to produce 4, and with 5 to produce 6.

Example 56

From the above example it can be seen that the two processes—finding the difference tones and summation tones of any interval—will lead to filling in the whole series of which that interval is a part, below the interval with difference tones and above it with summation tones. It is as though every interval casts its shadow above and below itself. The whole shadow is the same shape—that of the partial series—though its upper and lower boundaries are subject to the limits of our pitch perception.

We can get an idea of the complex pattern of frequencies resulting from a single interval by writing down *(1)* the partial series generated by each of the two real tones, limiting the range to the eighth partial for practical reasons; *(2)* the difference tones generated below the main notes; and *(3)* the summation tones.

There will be, of course, duplications between these three groups of pitches. But the total number of pitches represented will be, as said before, a good indication of the possible sensory effect upon the ear, and a measure of the complexities in comprehension.

Let us treat two intervals in this way and compare the results. We will choose the perfect fifth and the minor sixth.

Here is a tabulation of the results:

Example 57

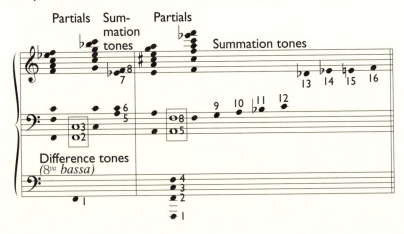

a. *Lowest coinciding partial.*
   Fifth. At partials 3 and 2.
   Minor sixth. At partials 6 and 5.
b. *Difference tones.*
   Fifth. The only difference tone supports the lower tone of the interval.
   Minor sixth. Of the four difference tones, three support the top note of the interval.
c. *Clashes.*
   Fifth. Clashes among the first eight partials occur between 5 and 3, 6 and 5, and 7 and 5.
   Minor sixth. Clashes among the first eight partials occur between 3 and 2, 5 and 3, 6 and 4, and 7 and 4.
d. *Summation tones.*
   Fifth. Only one summation tone lies above the senario (7). Summation tones double 6 and 5, and 8 and 7 an octave lower.
   Minor sixth. All summation tones lie above the senario. Summation tones begin with 9 and fill the space up to 16. There are clashes among the summation tones at 9, 11, 13, 14, and 15.
e. *Reinforcement.*
   Fifth. The lower tone is strongly reinforced as a root by the first order difference tone.
   Minor sixth. The upper note has strong support as root by three difference tones, but it is clouded in the octave above it by a *M7* (the third partial of the lower tone), and by summation tones which are not related to tones of the *senario.*

The net result of all the above comparisons does not change the relative positions of the fifth and minor sixth already established by the simpler comparison of the lower partials and the first few orders of difference tones, but the picture given by the summation tones of the minor sixth makes Franco of Cologne's judgment of it as dissonance even more understandable.

No one linear presentation can rank the intervals in a general hierarchy because a mixture of factors is involved; spatial factors in melodic use, blending or clashing partials in harmonic use, support or lack of it from difference tones, lower or upper tone supported as root, or no tone well supported as root. Nevertheless, the diagram below attempts to grade intervals from the octave to the tritone by showing them on two levels. The upper level has the intervals which have support for their lowest tone as root, and the lower level has intervals which have their top note supported as root. Leaving the octave and the tritone as unique, the segments separated by vertical lines show from left to right an increase of dissonance. If consonance and root support for the lower tone were positive factors, and dissonance and lack of root support for the lower tone were negative factors, the values could be read zig-zagging across the chart, as 8, 5, 4, *M3, m6, M2, M7, m2, T.*

Example 58

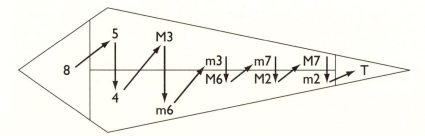

TONALITY

In the perception of intervals we have observed that our attention is directed to those tones which are supported by difference tone reinforcement. In most consonant intervals this support is undistracted by overtone clashes, so we have no problem in hearing that the lower note of the 5 and *M3* are prominent; or hearing that in the case of the 4 and *m6* the *weight* is on the upper tone.

Musical practice has supported such a concept: in polyphony the treatment of the fourth as requiring resolution to the third; the use of the $\frac{6}{4}$ chord to leave open the situation for a cadenza followed by resolution to a $\frac{5}{3}$; and many other cases in which the instability of an inverted interval is followed by the stability of one with its root below.

The tendency to rank one tone above another in the search for order among the tones has its parallel in the ranking of one tone above others in a succession of tones. In the horizontal dimension, difference tones have no part since they result only from sounding tones together in the vertical dimension. The tendency to pick out one tone above the others, to set up an hierarchical order, is not an acoustical phenomenon when tones are sounded in succession, but a psychological one. It appears to result from the mind's way of processing information (already mentioned) in which every impression is classified and ranked before filing it in the memory, or, as we say, *comprehending* it.

In a succession of tones, the one to receive the highest rank falls most easily to the first tone heard. That is, until the last tone is heard, in which case the first tone may have receded in memory, and the last tone remains without competition.

The importance of beginnings and endings in establishing the primacy of one tone (in this case, the final of a mode) was articulated with great clarity by "Odo of Cluny." Beginnings, too," he says, "are found most often and most suitably on the sound which concludes the melody."[7]

Another factor which may elevate a tone to prominence is repetition, especially if the tone is found prominently in the secondary endings which conclude phrases. Odo warns that repeated phrase endings on some tone other than the final could result in that other tone's usurping the place of the final.

> Several phrases ought to end with the sound which concludes the mode [the final], the masters teach, for if more endings be made in some other sound than be made in this one, they desire the melody to be ended in that other sound and compel it to be changed from the mode in which it was.[8]

While advantaged placement and repetition are the most direct way to impress one tone over the others in our perceptive consciousness, what we have learned in our experience with intervals sounded together may also build up the esteem held for certain intervals, and bring certain tones to a position of prominence. By such a carry-over from one realm of experience to another, the interval of a fifth may have a certain standing in situations where its smooth blending partials and its simple difference tone structure are not directly applicable. A tone standing in the *relationship* of a fifth to the main tones is perceived to have a close connection to it, and receives a rank next in order.

In the modal system, before any influence of harmony, the tone a fifth above the final held such rank *(dominant),* with certain exceptions having to do with avoidance of the tone b, notoriously connected to F by the infamous tritone.

The high rank of the tone a fifth above the main note in chant carries over to the period of harmonic practice; also added to it is the next most consonant interval, the fourth. Respect for fifth relationship becomes so great that the importance of the tone a fourth above the main note is explained by the circumstance that it also lies a fifth *below* the main note. Therefore, since the fifth is called *dominant,* the fourth is called *subdominant* (it is also one tone below the dominant in the scale).

The strength of closely connected intervals (the first steps in the Spatial Series) seem to have been realized in Western music only after the establishment of harmonic function. Endings from the half-step below the final are avoided in Gregorian chant, and are forbidden by Guido d'Arezzo in the converging endings *(occursus)* of early polyphony.[9]

Endings from the half-step above are not common in Gregorian chant because the modes in which they occur *(final, E)* are the least used. These same modes are declared by Guido to be "merely usable," not really well adapted to organum.

In harmonic practice, the binding effect of half-step progressions was utilized above all in the handling of the diatonic tritone. If one of its tones moved by a half-step upwards to the main note *(tonic),* all was well in the tonal world threatened by the untunable tritone.

The descending half-step from above the main note has a long history in melody outside the main stream of Western music; but it does not exist in the pattern of major or minor scales, it finds its way into harmonic practice only as an *altered* tone. One common use is in the *Neapolitan* chord which precedes a dominant chord in a cadence. The tones a half-step above and below circle the tonic before closing in on it.

Example 59

In music which is tonal but partly chromatic the descending half-step above the main note has been used as an important alternative to the ascending half-step in endings. A striking classical example is the ending of the last movement of Schubert's two-cello quintet.

Example 60

In the music of Paul Hindemith, who called the descending half step the *upper leading tone* (symbol:↓), there are hundreds of examples of such cadences, often with the descending progression in the bass.

Example 61a

Sonata for Violin and Piano (1939),
III, *Fugue*—last five measures.[10]

Example 61b

Requiem, "When lilacs last in the dooryard bloom'd."
3. March—three measures before Ⓐ.[11]

In several of the interval diagrams shown thus far we
have observed that the closest harmonic relationships lie at
one end of the diagram and the closest melodic relationships
at the other. That there is a polarity between harmonic and
melodic functions is pointed out by Hindemith in his description of what he calls the *main functions* of tonality.[12] These
are, of course, the tonic, dominant, subdominant and the two
leading tones. Substituting letters for some of Hindemith's
special symbols, this polarity is shown as follows, reading
from left to right with F as a tonic, and right to left with B as
a tonic.

Example 62

```
            ←─────────────
   Tr ↓ ↑        S  D  T
                    F♯
   F  C  B♭      E  G♭  B
         A♯
   T  D  S       ↑  ↓  Tr
            ─────────────→
```

The Blending Series given earlier (Example 49) shows this
same polarity between its first three and last three members.
An additional means of evaluating intervals can be found in
applying tonal analysis to them, i. e., assessing their possible
functions in the tonal hierarchy. As said before, the psycho-

logical search for the strongest interpretation of two (or more) tones results in root determination (vertical context) or tonic determination (horizontal context). Since we are to judge intervals in this case by functional possibilities, our scale of values must be based on both harmonic and melodic values. Example 58 above shows these values intermingled. If we assign numbers to weight the intervals by both harmonic and melodic criteria, we may set the octave (tonic) at 6, decreasing the harmonic values from 5 to 1, left to right, placing 1 at the minor third and *M6*. Setting the tritone at –6 to cancel the tonic (octave), we decrease the melodic values from 5 to 1, right to left, again arriving at 1 for the *m3* and *M6*.

That the *m3* and *M6* are at a neutral point in both harmonic and melodic value is consistent with what we have observed from their difference-tone profiles, which show them weak in root support; also neither interval has strong leading-tone possibilities.

Example 63

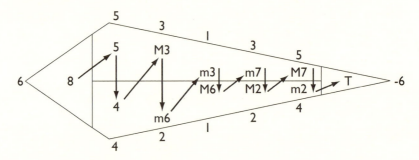

The functional possibilities of a specific interval may be examined as follows:

1. Take any two pitches, and assume in succession each of the twelve tones as tonic, assigning the function to each note according to that tonality.[13]

2. Using the chart above, assign to each note the weight indicated.

3. Add the numbers to derive the weight of the interval in the tonality chosen.

As an example, let us take the interval C–G, showing its possible functions in each of the twelve tonalities.

Example 64

Tonality	Functions	Weights	Total
C	D T	5 6	11
C♯	Tr ↑	-6 5	-1
D	5 m7	4 3	7
E♭	M3 M6	3 1	4
E	m3 m6	1 2	3
F	M2 D	2 5	7
F♯	↓ Tr	4 -6	-2
G	T S	6 4	10
A♭	↑ M3	5 3	8
A	m7 m3	3 1	4
B♭	M6 M2	1 2	3
B	M6 ↓	2 4	6

The tonality to which the interval most belongs is that which has the highest total weight according to the above method of measurement. It is to this interpretation that we turn first, and with the least effort. While it is possible to imagine a tonal connection to any of the possible tonalities, greater and greater effort is required as the interval's weight in the imagined tonality becomes less and less. The example below lists the interpretations of C–G in order of strength or tonal weight.

Example 65

C	11
G	10
A♭	8
D, F	7
B	6
E♭, A	4
B♭, E	3
C♯	-1
F♯	-2

All of the possible tonalities can be tested aurally by placing the interval in the context of a progression to the assumed tonic. The example below illustrates the relation of ·C–G to all the tonics.

Example 66

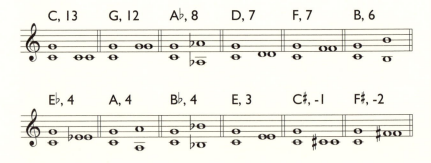

If we subject every interval to the test of tonal evaluation, finding the best possible interpretation of each one, we can arrive at another series that reveals still more of the individual *personality* of each interval.

The intervals can be grouped according to their functional tendencies; i. e., whether they have more of tonic-like characteristics (repose, suitable for stable points such as beginnings or endings), or dominant-like characteristics (energetic, suitable for on-going movement). Leading-tones strengthen either characteristic. Again, the *m3* and *M6* fall into a neutral zone; if one has a strong main function, the other has a weak one.

The series that results from these considerations—which are not acoustical in origin but psychological, the result of remembered and anticipated experiences—is as follows, using only main functions (T D S ↑ ↓).

Example 67

Functional Series

inactive ← ——————— ——————— → active

Tonic-like					Neutral		Dominant-like						
8	5	4	M7	m2	m3	M6	M3	m6	m7	M2		T	
T	D	T	↑	T	(m3)	T	↑	D	S	D	↑		D
T	T	D	T	↑	T	(m3)	D	↑	D	S	S		↓
					(m7)	D					S		↓
					D	(m7)					↑		D

4

Sonorities

DEFINITION OF SONORITY

O NE OF THE DIFFERENCES between traditional theory and twentieth century practice lies in the concept of *chord.* The traditional definition was clearly established by Rameau, and was held to without question until the last decades of the nineteenth century. In this definition, chords were units, not just combinations of intervals as they had been during the polyphonic period. Chords were built by superimposing thirds, they were invertible, and they moved from one to the other in coordination with the meter. Melody and polyphony grew upon a controlled foundation of chords.

While the twentieth century has continued to produce harmonically-generated music, one of its major thrusts has been to free chord construction from any fixed system of chord building such as superimposed thirds. Merely changing the interval of construction to fourths or any other single interval would remain just as rigid. A better new definition of *chord,* if one were to continue to use that term, would be: *any vertical group of three or more tones.*[1]

The concept of inversion is given up in favor of more general ways of determining whether the most important tone (the *root*) is in the bass or not. In situations where no one tone stands out as a root, contrapuntal factors take over, and root function is likely to become of secondary importance instead of being the primary means of regulating harmonic movement, as it was with the *basse fondamentale* of Rameau.[2]

In any case, all vertical combinations do produce a specific, if sometimes only momentary, aural effect. In order to disassociate these vertical events from the traditional concept of "chord," we shall call them *sonorities.*

In an interesting article, Walter Piston[3] shows certain vertical combinations in Bach which appear to be non-traditional in shape. He then reveals that they occur through the use of melodic ornamentation and rhythmic devices of anticipation and suspension. Such groups of notes may not be chords, but they are *sonorities,* and they have a certain aural effect no matter how their occurrence is explained by the manipulations of traditional theory.

In serial composition, every tone may be theoretically justified by its place within the row, but the vertical sounds assert themselves independently of any reasoning that may have caused them to occur. However, only the most rigid serial or extra-musical method will leave the composer *no* room for choosing one tone over another, or the place it is to occur. If the composer is to have such a choice, he cannot default by treating all combinations as equally suitable in any situation; he must exercise his right to choose the tones he prefers. A multiplicity of such choices will ultimately reveal something of the composer's personality as surely as a Rorschach test. A decision to use methods which exclude choice would in itself convey a message.

To make choices from among the enormous variety unleashed by the general definition of "any vertical group of three or more tones," we need some means of classification into broad groups according to important characteristics of sonorities.[4]

A sonority will involve at least three tones and the three

intervals formed between them; the aural effect will be determined by the interval content (contextual factors are not considered here).

Intervals are classified into consonances and dissonances. The former are further subdivided into perfect and imperfect consonances. The latter are not usually subdivided in traditional classification, but here we shall classify the minor seventh and major second as *soft* dissonances, and the major seventh and minor second as *hard* dissonances. The tritone is a dissonance in its own class, and the octave is a consonance in its own class.

CLASSIFICATION OF SONORITIES: SYMBOLS

We need symbols to avoid having to give complete verbal descriptions of the interval characteristics of each sonority. For the components so far described, we may use a circle divided into halves and quarters.

The upper right hand quadrant represents the perfect consonances, fifth and fourth. The lower right hand quadrant represents the imperfect consonances, thirds and sixths.

The upper left hand quadrant represents the soft dissonances, minor seventh and major second. The lower left hand quadrant represents the hard dissonances, major seventh and minor second. The left hand side of the circle contains all dissonances except the tritone.

Example 68

The tritone is shown by a small circle drawn around the cross point of the quadrants in the middle of the ball.

Example 69

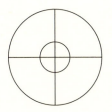

If chromaticism is present, a short line (to the right or left) is drawn across the center of the ball at the cross point.

Example 70

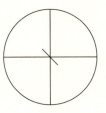

If the intervals of one quadrant are not present, that quadrant is left uncircled.

Example 71

If two quadrants on one side of the ball are missing, the two quadrants that remain do not have to be encircled.

Example 72

If the two quadrants at opposite corners are represented, a diagonal line is drawn from the upper to lower or lower to upper corners, and there is no encirclement.

Example 73

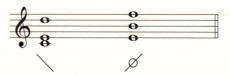

The only quadrant which alone can represent three different notes is the lower right (thirds and sixths). There are only two such sonorities; one contains a tritone and the other is chromatic.

Example 74

To demonstrate the use of the symbols, let us examine some of the known sonorities of traditional harmony.

Example 75

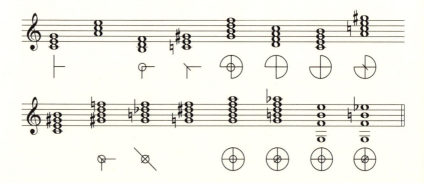

Note that inversions do not change the symbol, since sym-

bols only show the interval content. The same is true with
open spacing.

The symbols can reveal the kinship between some traditional chord shapes and non-traditional ones.

Example 76

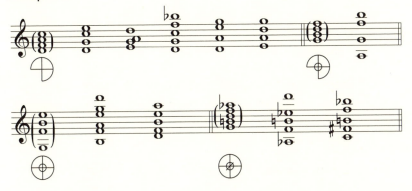

The symbols may also help to reveal groups of sonorities
which fit together homogeneously, and to define the limits of
the kinds of sonorities which can be achieved by a given
number of tones. For example, with three tones there are the
usual triads shown in the example above, all of which come
from the right side of the ball; but there are also the following possibilities:

Example 77

Three-note sonorities can express only two quadrants;
also, either a tritone or chromaticism can be present, but not
both. In any three-note sonority, two or three characteristic
ingredients will be missing. Each of the six ingredients con-

tributes a certain quality to the sonority. At the risk of becoming subjective, we may describe these qualities as follows:

1. Upper right *(4, 5)*. Power of projection, resonance, strength.
2. Lower right *(3, 6)*. Color, fullness, richness
3. Upper left *(M2, m7)*. More color, mild tension.
4. Lower left *(M7, m2)*. Intensified color, sharper tension.
5. Tritone *(O)*. A special characteristic of unrest or tonal instability, its effect depending on the other intervals placed with it.
6. Chromaticism *(X)*. The highest degree of color and tonal instability, again depending for its effect on the other intervals placed with it.

The four chromatic formulas have different characteristics resulting from their interval content:

1. *Mm*—a high degree of color because of the prismatic splitting of the third; intensity because a minor second is involved.
2. *TT*—increases the instability but not the dissonant intensity (noise factor) unless minor seconds are involved. Multiple tritones and minor seconds form the sharpest sonorities.
3. *MM*—the mildest chromatic sonority. High degree of color, very low projection. Gains intensity in the presence of *M7–m2;* dissolves into whole-tone structure with *m7–M2.*
4. *HH*—this formula adds intensity (noise factor) to other groups of intervals. By itself, it has only the quality of noise—no color or projection. Combined with fifths or fourths, but without thirds or sixths, the sonority is both forceful in

projection and harsh. The presence of a third
adds color to balance the intensity.

Example 78

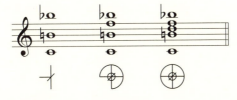

While it is possible to have three-note sonorities with or
without dissonances or the tritone or chromaticism, all four-
note sonorities must have a dissonance, the mildest ones being from the upper left quadrant *(m7–M2)*.

The symbol ⊕ accounts for a very large number of four-
note sonorities which in a dissonant style qualify as consonant, taking the place occupied by triads in the traditional
style which alternates consonance and dissonance. To any of
these sonorities, a fifth note may be added without changing
the symbol.

Example 79

These sonorities are, in fact, pentatonic, in that they have
no half-steps, tritones or chromaticism, and could be formed
from the notes of a pentatonic scale. The terms, pentatonic,
diatonic and chromatic, used earlier to categorize groups of
scales, may also categorize groups of sonorities. A diatonic
sonority is one that displays interval characteristics which
cannot occur in pentatonicism, but which are not chromatic.
A chromatic sonority is one that contains one or more chromatic formulas.

Designations of sonorities according to the above categories may reveal information about tension levels different
from that found by counting dissonant clashes produced by
seconds. For example, in the following juxtapositions of two
sonorities there is a drop in tension from Sonority 1 to Sonority 2, though Sonority 2 contains seconds and Sonority 1 does
not. The drop in tension occurs because there is a drop in *category* from chromatic to pentatonic, which cannot be balanced by the addition of seconds in Sonority 2.

Example 80

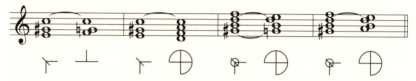

The above explanation by categories is a simplification of
the actual acoustical situation. All chromatic formulas produce a complex difference tone picture which pentatonic
groupings do not. The following example shows the difference tones generated by the two sonorities in the first of the
above progressions. The drop in complexity between Sonority
1 and Sonority 2 is graphically clear in the boxed-in segments, which combine the sounding notes with the difference
tones generated by each of their intervals.

Example 81

Six-note sonorities must contain at least one half-tone, if not a tritone. They are hexatonic or diatonic at least, but they may also contain *O* or *X*, or both. Their tension will depend on whatever intervals combine with the inevitable minor second.

Example 82

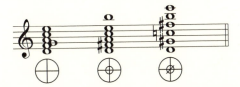

Seven-note sonorities must contain at least one tritone. The seven-note sonority with one tritone but no chromatic formula is the saturated diatonic chord. Its static quality results from the fact that the sonority contains both the tritone and its tonic resolution. If this tone (the *11th*) is omitted (as it is in traditional usage), what remains is a dominant chord with *7th, 9th* and *13th*.

Example 83

In the pandiatonic style of neo-classicism (when every combination of the diatonic notes was sought, especially the two dissonant half-steps), combinations of tonic and dominant often fell together, producing harmonies containing both the leading-tone and its tonic resolution. Those in which the tonic is the lower of the two notes (forming a *M7*) are much less harsh than those with the tonic above the leading-tone (forming a minor ninth).

Example 84

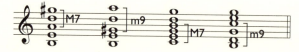

If any other note is added to the seven-note diatonic chord, the result is chromaticism in one or more of its formulas. The chord symbols become useless at this point since all six ingredients are present: the four quadrants and *O* and *X*. The saturation chord would be the one containing all twelve pitches—a remarkable sound in good spacing, but as useless in construction as a twelve ton block of stone.

Example 85

Of course, it does not require all twelve pitches, or even eight pitches, to invoke all the components of the complete sonority symbol; as few as four tones may do so. In this sort of situation, it may be appropriate to omit repeating the symbols and simply note the chromatic formulas that are used. In very dissonant sonorities, it may be well to note the number of harsh dissonances from the lower right quadrant *(M7–m2)*.

Example 86

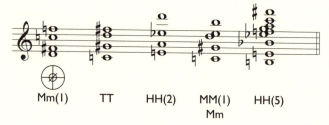

ROOTS OF SONORITIES

We have seen that intervals may have roots when the difference tones support one tone more strongly than the other. The same phenomenon occurs with sonorities, which are combinations of intervals.[5]

To take the simplest case first, a major triad in fundamental form has three intervals: a *M3* and a *5* above the lowest tone, and a minor third between the middle tone and the upper tone. In the example below, the numbers to the left of each note are its numbers in the partial series. The darkened notes are the difference tones.

Example 87

One can see from the above illustration that the lower note of a major triad in fundamental form is overwhelmingly supported as the most prominent note in the sonority, and it is therefore the root.

The root of a major triad remains the same when it is inverted.

Example 88

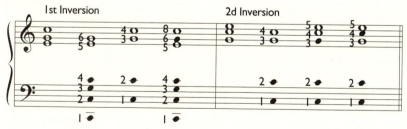

Note that the second inversion, since its lowest tone is a third partial, has fewer difference tones than the first inversion, in which the lowest tone is a fifth partial.

The lowest tone of a sonority has an advantage over the others when it comes to being heard as a root. The fact that it *is* the lowest note enables it to be singled out more easily. Also, since each tone of the sonority sends up its own partial series, the lowest one has the spot least likely to be clouded by partials from other tones, a situation which occurs frequently in widely-spaced sonorities. Only strong evidence to the contrary (such as the difference tones occurring in the examples above) can force the attention to a note located above the bass tone of a sonority.

If we examine the minor triad, we see that even in its uninverted form, its lower tone is not as clearly supported in its root function as was the lower tone of a major triad.

Example 89

Counting the difference tones (darkened notes), we can observe that *C–E♭* has four: three *A♭*s and one *E♭*. *C–G* has one which supports *C*. *E♭–G* has three: two *E♭*s and one *B♭*. *A♭* has the largest representation (3), and is supported also by *E♭* (2); furthermore, it is the lowest pitch within the complex. The only basis for calling *C* the root of this minor triad is that it is the lowest *sounding note,* while its competitor is only a difference tone.

The inversions of the minor triad reveal a different situation, one long observed in harmonic practice. The lower tone of the first inversion of a minor triad can assume the function of a root because it has priority of position, and it is supported well by difference tones.

Example 90

Though the II^6 chord is called the first inversion of the supertonic triad, its use before the V in cadences has long been equated with the subdominant (IV), which, in fact, is its bass tone. The subdominant impression is even stronger when the chord has its seventh, as in II$^6_3$. The bass tone is then supported by its fifth. In either form, C, with its high position in the chord, cannot compete with $E\flat$ for priority as a root tone.

Example 91

In the second inversion of the minor triad, $E\flat$ is in a less good position, and its strongest interval (now the lowest one) has the root C. The bass tone, G, cannot be the root because it is subordinate to C in the interval of a fourth, which has strong first and second order difference tones.

Though C does remain the root of the second inversion of the minor triad, this chord, like its fundamental form, presents a much more complicated picture than its parallel in major (compare the difference tone diagrams).

Example 92

2d inversion

Though the full picture of a sonority would need to show all the difference tones generated by each of its intervals (and to be complete, all the partials generated by each of its tones), shorter methods of finding the root tone, if any, can be used which take for granted what is already known about the roots of intervals, combining that information with the priorities of placement.

We know that the *5, M3, 4,* and *m6* are the intervals most strongly supported by difference tones, and that the *m3* and *M6* are not well supported. Sevenths and seconds, by themselves, will seldom be the crucial intervals to support a root, but together with thirds or fifths they may lend additional support. The exception to this statement is that a seventh (especially the minor seventh) as the lower two notes in a sonority, will support its lowest tone as root against any competition from all pitches lying in a higher register.

FUNCTIONAL ANALYSIS

As we have said before, in any calculation of roots, the initial assumption should be that the lowest tone is a root unless proven otherwise. Most likely to shift the root away from the lowest tone would be the note lying just above it, if that note has strong difference tone support. This event may occur when the lowest interval in the sonority is a fourth or minor sixth. A fifth, major third, or minor seventh as the lowest interval practically insure the bass tone as root.

Musical practice has long recognized these realities. The special treatment of the fourth above the bass, from the polyphonic era through the period of common practice, was in recognition of that interval's power to usurp the power of the bass tone. The avoidance of the fifth as the lower interval in non-tonal chromatic polyphony acknowledges that interval's ability to focus too much attention on the bass note, and to create roots in a kind of polyphony that does not rely on root progression as a basis for harmonic movement.

Just as with intervals, when we applied the test of tonal functions as an aid in determining the most important tone, we can apply functional analysis to sonorities.[6] In simple cases, this method will only show what difference tone analysis has already shown. For example, the best functional analysis of the uninverted major triad, *C–E–G,* is tonic-major third-dominant. The tonic *(T)* is the strongest function; that note by the other method is called the root. That the root has changed positions is clear in the in the inversions: *M3–D–T,* or *D–T–M3.*

By contrast, in the case of the augmented triad no one of its tones is well supported by difference tones. In this sort of situation (and with most sonorities involving tritones and/or chromaticism), functional analysis can be helpful. The following example shows the augmented triad *C–E–G♯.* The best form of this sonority would be the one which gives the lowest note the best possible function. This can only be the dominant, since the augmented fifth defeats any intention to regard it as a tonic. Treating the lowest tone as a dominant yields three respellings of the sonority.

Example 93

$\text{a: } \mathrm{III}^{6\natural}_{3\sharp}$ $\text{f: } \mathrm{III}^{6\flat}_{3\natural}$ $\text{C}\sharp\text{: } \mathrm{III}^{6\natural}_{3\sharp}$

The dominant, being the highest ranking function and occupying the privileged place at the bottom of the sonority, becomes a *surrogate* root, though lacking acoustical support.

The above analysis is supported in traditional practice by the not uncommon substitution of the III^6 in minor for the dominant, since that tone is present in the bass, and the melodic function of the leading-tone is present.

That the augmented triad is treated as a dissonance in traditional theory though it consists entirely of consonances can be partially explained by the complex pattern of difference tones it produces.

Example 94

Other three-note sonorities which have ambiguous roots may be analyzed according to functional possibilities. For example:

Example 95

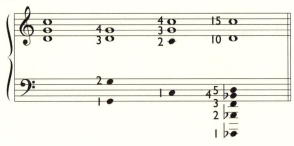

The first interval, *D–G,* supports *G;* the second interval, *G–C,* supports *C;* and the third interval, *D–C,* has the weak support of a 1st order difference tone for *D,* and a rich collection of difference tones (characteristic for any dissonance) supporting *B♭. D* has some priority because of its position as the lowest note, and on that basis it might be treated as a root—though *G* draws some strength from it, while *C* draws some strength from *G.* Functional analysis, however, shows that the note of highest tonal value (therefore, root) is *G.* The triad in the form of superimposed fourths is consequently an inversion, the fundamental form (root in the bass) being *G–C–D.*

Example 96

Chords that do not contain acoustically supported roots will present possible leading-tone functions. The best combination of leading-tone with other functional degrees will be the most probable analysis, and the leading-tone so indicated will be the surrogate root.

For example, let us analyze the traditional diminished seventh chord, so famous for its ambiguity and lack of an acoustically supported root (some theorists have said that it is the ninth chord without its root, assuming that it must have had one). Here are analyses which interpret each tone of the sonority as an ascending leading tone (↑).

Example 97

The tonal weight for this sonority is the same for each interpretation, but the one giving the best function to the lowest tone is in *A;* therefore *G♯* is the highest ranking note, or surrogate root. The next most satisfactory interpretation places the leading-tone in the top voice. Those placing the leading-tone in the middle voices, where it is not so easily perceived, produce less believable resolutions of this chord.

Even more distant relationships can be assigned to the diminished seventh chord by the assumption that one of its tones is a *descending* leading-tone. Because the other note of the tritone is then a dominant, the tonal weight of this interpretation is actually higher than that assuming an ascending leading-tone.

Judged melodically, the best interpretation is the one that places the leading tone in the top voice.

Example 98

The tonal ambiguity of the diminished seventh chord is eliminated by the addition of any other note below it (i. e., any pitch not contained in the chord). These notes, of which there are eight, will form a fifth or fourth with one of the notes of the chord. Those that form a fifth will produce the dominant group, *D–↑–S,* with one of the tritones in the chord. The lowest note of the chord will be a dominant and the root.

Example 99

Those tones that form a fourth will give the impression of a tonic pedal below the tritone, $S-\uparrow$. The lowest note of the chord will be a tonic and the root.

Example 100

Of the traditional diatonic seventh chords in major, only two contain the tritone: the V^7 and the VII^7.

The V^7 responds perfectly to both difference tone analysis and functional analysis. Its lower note is the root of the major triad to which the seventh has been added, and the same root is retained in all three inversions. The tritone's function as S is firmly defined by the dominant which is the root of the chord.

Example 101

It is no accident of history or consequence of conditioning that has caused the movement of this sonority to the one which has the tonic as its root to have been the linch-pin of musical structures in a long and productive segment of Western music.

The VII^7 does not have a root in fundamental form because there is a tritone above its lowest tone. In the first inversion, with a fifth as its lowest interval, it does have a strong root.

Example 102

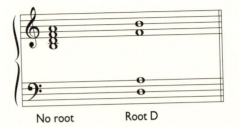

No root   Root D

In its fundamental form and in other inversions, the tritone predominates, and the main consideration is the establishment of its function.

If in the context a *G* is nearby, then the tritone can be defined in relation to a *C* tonic, and the sonority acquires an active, forceful character.

If *G♯* is nearby, the tritone relationship it forms with *D* of the chord dominates the *F–B,* and the latter tritone becomes non-functional and quiescent.

Example 103

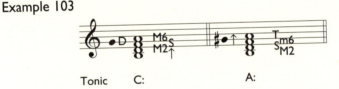

Tonic   C: A:

In tonal value, the two interpretations shown above have nearly the same weight; but in *C* the sonority is more active because of its leading-tone (melodic value), while in *A* it is more stable because it contains a tonic (harmonic value).

It was pointed out earlier (see Example 91) that the addition of a fifth above the bass to the first inversion of a minor triad strengthens that bass tone's function as a root. The chord in the example, called II^6 in *B♭* (first inversion of the seventh chord on the supertonic) is an inversion only on paper, made by the scheme of constructing chords through the superimposition of thirds. According to that method, the lowest note of the pyramid of thirds would be *C*, and therefore *C* is designated as the root. But taking the difference tones formed by this sonority into account, and by acknowledging the priorities of the lowest tone and the lowest interval, the most prominent sound (and therefore the *sounding root*) may be some tone other than the one from which the chord was generated, which we may call the *schematic root*.

As it turns out, among traditional harmonies the capability of keeping the same root after all inversions belongs only to the major triad and to the seventh chord formed by adding a minor seventh to it (V^7). In all the *secondary sevenths* not containing a tritone or chromaticism (II, III, VI in major and VI in minor), the schematic root on which the chord was built may be replaced upon inversion by another tone with better support, depending on the disposition of the tones in the middle and top of the sonority. The following example will illustrate this principle. The darkened notes are the sounding roots.

Example 104

$$\text{II}^6_5 \qquad {}^4_3 \qquad {}^4_2 \qquad \text{I}^6_5 \qquad {}^4_3 \qquad {}^4_2$$

The numbers in figured bass were never intended to indicate the *distribution* of tones above the bass. However, we can observe that as long as the tones $^6_3$, $^4_3$, and $^4_2$ retain their vertical order, the root of the original chord (the schematic root) is also the sounding root. Where the tones are inverted to $^5_6$, $^3_4$, and $^2_3$, the sounding root shifts from the lowest tone of the inverted chord to the third of that chord.

The above examples show that root invertibility was not a

consistently held characteristic even of the harmonies of traditional usage; and therefore it would have even less chance of being a viable principle in more complex non-traditional sonorities. Also, the idea of building chords by successively imposing any one interval has no more than schematic usefulness, whether the interval is a third, fourth, second, or any other interval; nor could the starting point of such constructions, though schematically the root, retain its importance if moved into the upper regions of complex sonorities.

In the light of all the above, we arrive back where we started: defining a sonority (chord) simply as three or more tones sounded together, and relying on no symmetrical method of construction.

The tones of a sonority make combinations of intervals, and the character of the sonority will depend on its interval content. The grading of intervals on the basis of blending or clashing partials, difference tones, and functional possibilities in tonal thinking provide some information, all of which considered together may help to determine the effect of a multi-interval sonority.

Though each sonority has to be evaluated on its own terms, certain broad categories can be defined. The first categories are established by interval content. For these categories, we have the six ingredients defined by the sonority symbols, *4–5, 3–6, m7–M2,* tritone, and chromaticism.

Another factor concerns roots. What is the most prominent tone, if any? Is it the bass tone, or does it lie higher in the sonority? Root determination may also involve tonal evaluation. What are the best possible functional interpretations? What expectations are created by the act of tonal thinking? Is the tonic present in the chord or only anticipated?

No simple chart will guide a composer through the vast sea of possible sonorities made available by the sweeping definition which includes every combination of three or more tones. Only detailed consideration of every factor will define the sonorities and whether they fit the situation in which they occur or whether they need to be modified.

Trial and error has been a hallowed procedure of composition in the past, and rules of thumb have saved some labor. It is hoped that the types of analysis shown here may help the composer in mustering information on which to base his own rules of thumb, and to shorten both his trials and his errors.

BUILDING SONORITIES

The previous discussion of sonorities appears to treat them as though they were musical objects in themselves, without concern as to how they might be formed, or how they might occur in context. It is only in Western music that such a preoccupation with simultaneous sounds could exist; no other music, if there are coincidences of more than one pitch, pays any attention to them. It is very much in the Western tradition to do so; sonorities have been a main concern from the beginnings of polyphony through the various style periods up to the present.

In the early stages of polyphony, the sonorities were only perfect consonances, regulated by a theory closely linked to late Greek ideas of consonance, and supported by demonstrations on the monochord. With the addition of a third independent voice (rarely, a fourth voice) towards the end of the twelfth and the beginning of the thirteenth century, the sonorities were built up voice by voice, and controlled by the use of consonances on all the main metric points. This same method of layered construction gradually admitted imperfect consonances, and by the time of the Renaissance, full three-note sonorities expressed in four or more parts were more frequent than sonorities made from combinations of only fifths, fourths and octaves.

By 1722 (the date of Rameau's *Traité de l'harmonie*) the modes had been reduced to two, defined by their major or minor thirds, and were available in twelve keys. Chords were formed as prearranged units by superimposing thirds upon a fundamental. A major third and a minor third added together produced the "perfect chord," which by delightful coincidence existed in the newly-discovered partial series. To that a seventh or ninth could be added. These chord units (except for the ninth) were considered to be fully invertible.

Whereas polyphonic music had relied on the conformity of all the voices to the mode to take care of the movement of one sonority to another and to guarantee cohesion between all the sonorities, Rameau proposed to regulate the movement of his chords from one to the other by the progression of chord roots (i. e., the schematic roots on which the chords were based). The roots formed an unsounded, though perceived, line called the *basse fondamentale.*

In the post-Rameau definition of sonority stated here, building by thirds or any other one interval is no longer the basis, and the roots of sonorities are not those that refer to a pre-arranged shape, but rather those determined by a variety of factors. Also, there are sonorities which have no clear root.

Therefore, movement from sonority to sonority can be controlled by the fundamental bass (which Hindemith calls "root-progression") only when the sonorities have clear roots; otherwise, forward movement is determined by the bass line.

Strong melodic functions (leading-tones) may be, in some cases, more important in the connection of sonorities than root movement.

The selection of pitches is now no longer from the modes or the major and minor scales, but from the whole chromatic supply. In tonal chromatic music, attention is directed to certain pitches, thereby creating an hierarchical organization in which tonal functions are clear. In non-tonal chromatic music, emphasis on any one pitch is avoided and tonal functions are negated. Order consists not in maintaining an hierarchy but in achieving a balance which distributes the tones in a way to prevent one from dominating the others.

Whether the chromatic style is a free one, partially or fully chromatic, serial, or in some other way organized to assure an even flow of chromatic pitches, some vertical combinations are likely to occur—unless the piece is for a solo, wind instrument or voice—and these sonorities can be analyzed, judged, and modified by the procedures outlined in this chapter.

Construction that *begins* with vertical groups of pitches may make even better use of individual analysis of sonorities than the linear methods that form them additively. However, the result of homophonic procedures in chromatic music may lead to over-simplification as it does in tonal music. Polyphonic procedures are always likely to insure a higher degree of randomicity, no matter how tightly controlled is the technique.

5
Chromatic Modes

THE PARTIAL SERIES VS. THE CIRCLE OF FIFTHS

EVER SINCE PROOF of the existence of overtones, and the realization that the theory of intervals (long known in mathematics and on the monochord) had a natural basis in the partial vibrations of a single tone, attempts have been made to find connections between this structure given to us by nature and the structures of music theory.

The first and most joyous discovery was that the major triad, already hallowed by centuries of practice, was conspicuously present near the beginning of the series. The biggest disappointment was that the minor triad was not to be found among these tone-groupings. Also, the fundamental had a fifth (twelfth) as its third partial, but no fourth. These two circumstances made it difficult to connect the partial series to a theory which relied on major and minor triads and the strength of the fifth and fourth as dominant and subdominant.

A way out was to postulate an *undertone* series in which the subdominant occurs below the fundamental, and the minor triad appears as the reverse construction of the major triad—*m3–M3* instead of *M3–m3*. However, nothing in the nature of sound suggests the existence of undertones, though

108

in arithmetic the number one may be divided as well as multiplied.

The presence of the whole major triad in the partial series proved to be a dangerously seductive fact, in that it led to a search for other whole units of music in the series; whereas, what the series actually gives us is a sequence of numerical *proportions,* which alone or in combination can provide us with models for all tonal structures.

True enough, the tone a fourth above the fundamental is not to be found in the lower partials, but the *proportion* of a fourth, 3:4, is there with the fundamental as its upper tone (two octaves up).

As for the minor triad, it also does not occur directly over the fundamental, but the proportions of the intervals which comprise it (5:6, 4:5, 2:3) are present.

Since the partial series is the expression of division from larger to smaller parts in arithmetical progression, there can be no direct model for a scale containing similar-sized intervals, such as are needed for melody. The only approximation in the partial series of notes not too far apart or too close together for scale-like melody is in the region above the seventh partial, which can be produced on some brass instruments. These steps are unequal, of course, the lower ones being too large and the upper ones too small for a whole-tone. On the natural trumpet, at least a portion of a scale can be formed from *8–9–10–11–12* by lip alteration, making *11* flat enough to approximate a half-step with *10.*

The utilization of the partial series for musical construction, then, cannot rely on direct appropriation of "natural" groupings, but it can take the intervals themselves and combine them in normal or modified form to produce whatever is needed for horizontal (melodic) or vertical (harmonic) construction.

Although the series itself consists of proportional relationships of continuously different sizes, any closed musical system has to be built of a smaller number of sizes; and there should also be the possibility of interchangeable units of the same size, similar to replaceable parts in manufacture.

The octave is no candidate for building a musical system, since it clones itself over and over again. But the fifth, can produce new pitches when it is superimposed over and over up to the point the starting note is reached seven octaves higher. As we have seen, this circle (or spiral) is not truly closed but exceeds the octave by the Pythagorean comma. The fourth may also be made into a twelve-note circle, but it will fall short of the starting point five octaves higher, also by a Pythagorean comma.

Six whole-tones of 8:9 (the difference between a fifth and fourth) will exceed the octave by a Pythagorean comma.

The margin by which fifths, fourths, or the whole-tone 8:9 exceed or fall short of the octave is far less than the error produced by other intervals. Here are the results produced by major and minor thirds and the small whole-tone, 9:10.

$$\begin{aligned}
&\text{Major third (4:5)} && 386 \times 3 = 1158 \text{ Error: } -42 \\
&\text{Minor third (5:6)} && 316 \times 3 = 1264 \text{ Error: } +64 \\
&\text{Major second (9:10)} && 182 \times 6 = 1092 \text{ Error: } -108
\end{aligned}$$

We see from the above, then, that the use of fifths in finding pitches to fill the octave is not an arbitrary choice but a practical one, long appreciated by theorists concerned with organizing the musical material.[1]

SYMMETRICAL ORDERING OF THE TWELVE TONES

Having once derived the twelve tones through successive operations, we placed them in the conventional chromatic scale format, lowest tone to highest. This format, however, shows no connection to the order of derivation, nor does it reveal any of the interesting symmetries which are inherent in any natural order, whether tones, leaf patterns or crystals. The following diagram places the generating tone in the center of the lowest of three staves, and its opposing tritone on the highest staff above it. On the middle staff are the other tones in the order of their derivation, from left to right. The intervals formed by each pitch[2] with the generating tone are indicated by symbols.

Example 105

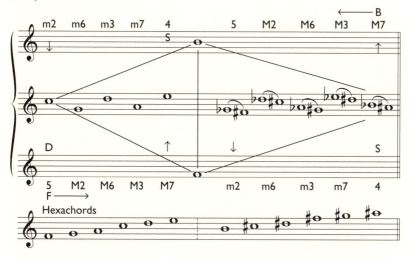

Observe the following features of the above diagram:

1. On the middle staff, to the left are the tones of the first hexachord on *F;* to the right are the tones of the complementary hexachord on *B.*

2. If B is taken as the generating tone instead of *F,* the first hexachord is on the right side, and the complementary hexachord is on the left. This demonstrates the polarity of the tritone relationship; if *F* is positive, *B* is negative; if *B* is positive, *F* is negative.

3. Intervals and their inversions occupy similar places on the two sides of the diagram. If an inverted interval is on the right, its inversion occu-

pies a similar place on the left, and vice versa.

4. The polarity of the fifth and fourth (dominant and subdominant), and the half-steps above and below the generator (upper and lower leading tones) is demonstrated. If F is the generator, the dominant and subdominant are at opposite ends (left and right), and the leading-tones are in the middle next to the generator. If B is the generator, the leading-tones are at opposite ends, and the dominant and subdominant are in the middle. The order of these relationships (right or left) is reversed between those related to F and those related to B.

Besides the features noted above, this diagram shows concisely what we have already observed in the operations of finding the tones: it follows the growth path of musical systems from pentatonic to chromatic.

Joseph Yasser has pointed out that musical systems grow according to a Fibonacci series.[3] Applied in this context, the series works as follows: representing the first fifth by 2, we add three more tones to the system (by superimposing fifths) to reach the five-tone level, two more to bring it to the seven-tone level; and five more to bring it to the twelve-tone level. The pattern is:

$$2 + 3 = 5$$
$$5 + 2 = 7$$
$$7 + 5 = 12$$

This series has been used in the theory of division of the octave. Its continuation leads to:

$$12 + 7 = 19$$
$$19 + 12 = 31$$

Vicentino (1555) constructed an archicembalo with thirty-one keys in six banks, which offered thirty-one fifths tempered to 697 cents (approximately the Meantone fifth), and natural major thirds. Joseph Yasser proposed a nineteen-tone tempered keyboard which included natural minor thirds.

Vicentino's keyboards could achieve better intonation from all twelve starting points by making alternate pitches available to eliminate the "Wolf" intervals. Yasser was able to provide large and small chromatic steps (126.3 and 63.2) to escape the equal-spaced chromatic scale of the tempered twelve-note system.

The resulting modes (twelve of them by the formula that the number of modes equals the number of tones in a single mode) could be performed on any one of nineteen starting points (the number of starting points, or keys, equals the number of pitches within the octave).

The fact that nineteen and thirty-one are along the track of better solutions to the temperament problem, and that theoretical proposals involving these numbers lead to more satisfactory results than, for example, the arbitrary splitting of twelve into twenty-four (quarter tones), suggests that 2–5–7–12–19–31 is indeed a basic series that reveals itself significantly in tones. It is one of the mathematical shadows behind the complex pattern of musical evolution in man's culture.

We have seen that much effort, expended over a number of centuries, was required to establish an octave with twelve chromatic pitches. The territory was conquered to provide space in which our seven-tone system could move around in different areas. But at this point, familiarity has made the different areas coalesce into one larger space now occupied not by a population of seven moving from area to area, but a population of twelve filling the whole area, as it were. Since movement to different areas is not possible without defining more spaces within the octave (such as with a nineteen-tone keyboard), the available space must be divided equally, and movement will have to consist of *exchange of places* between the occupants.

CHROMATIC MODES (UNMIXED)

Taking the situation as it is, then, we must separate the twelve pitches into mutually exclusive groups of six (hexachords). The above diagram (Example 105) illustrates this division, the first hexachord being on F, which we may designate as positive, and the second on its tritone, B, which we may designate as negative. A fully chromatic music would have to use all of both hexachords to maintain a balance between positive and negative. Of course, partly chromatic music is possible also; the diatonic scales contain the six positive tones and one negative one (the tritone), and there are five additional negative tones which could be added before the six and six balance is reached. While we do not have the possibility of chromatic modes with patterns of large and small half-steps such as the nineteen-tone temperament would provide, there are many other possibilities resulting from exchange of positions between the tones of the first (positive) and second (negative) hexachords. Further, there are six modal forms of the positive hexachord, with six corresponding negative hexachords.

Before we place the positive and negative hexachords together to form twelve-tone modes, let us examine in more detail the structure of the hexachords.

Within the modal hexachords there are three kinds of melodic steps: the whole-tone (W), the half-tone (H), and the minor third (the large step of pentatonicism). Each modal hexachord consists of two *trichords* with a pair of melodic steps. Each trichord is separated from the others by a whole-step.

Here are the positive Hexachords 1, 2, and 3, showing the structure of the trichords.

Example 106

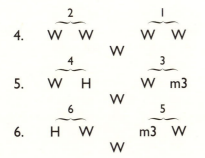

The patterns of positive Hexachords 4, 5, and 6 are as follows:

Example 107

It can be observed that Hexachords 4, 5, and 6 have the same trichords as 1, 2, and 3, but in reverse order.

Now let us examine the structure of the negative hexachords. Those that lie at the interval of a tritone from the positive hexachord have the same trichord structure. But if the negative pitches are placed at half-step intervals from the positive pitches, bringing the whole chromatic mode within the span of one octave, thereby causing the negative pitches to "map into" the positive ones, the negative hexachords have the reverse pattern of trichords. That is to say, the negative hexachord of Mode 1 has the same pattern as the positive hexachord of Mode 4. The same relationship exist between Modes 2 and 5, and 3 and 6.

Example 108

The Chromatic Modes

Shown above are the six unmixed chromatic modes, i. e., those in which the positive and negative tones remain in mutually exclusive hexachords, placed in what we shall call Frames 1 and 2, separated by a dotted barline. The form used is that which places the positive and negative tones within one chromatic octave.

CHROMATIC MODES (MIXED)

Every combination of twelve pitches is reducible to one of the above modes, if the positive and negative tones are restored to their original hexachords in Frames 1 and 2. Conversely, from these chromatic modes, all combinations of twelve tones can be built up by mixing the positive and negative pitches from opposite frames in varying degrees. Such mixtures may occur in the following proportions:

Example 109

Frame 1		Frame 2	
Positive	Negative	Positive	Negative
5	1	1	5
4	2	2	4
3	3	3	3
2	4	4	2
1	5	5	1

The sonorous effect of the twelve tones consisting of the unmixed hexachords is diatonic to the maximum degree. Many diatonic (tonal) groupings will occur in the melodic lines and in the vertical sonorities. The melodic structures tend to fall into two alternating diatonic areas; the contrapuntal effect when the two hexachords are combined is chromatic, but under certain conditions of registration or scoring, unmixed hexachords give a clear impression of bitonality.

The maximum chromatic effect occurs when the positive and negative tones are contained equally in both frames, the 3–3 mixture.

The last two combinations in the above diagram, 2–4, 4–2, and 1–5, 5–1, are no different in effect from the first two, 5–1, 1–5, and 4–2, and 2–4.

These schemes, of course, do not indicate *which* tones are displaced, only how many. There are numerous combinations—too many to fruitfully list them all.

The choice of tones to form a twelve-tone row or set goes beyond theoretical scheming such as we have attempted here and enters into the realm of compositional decision, for which theory can be helpful in pointing out possibilities, but never in directing taste.

REDUCTIONS OF TWELVE-TONE ROWS

Having suggested that any group of twelve pitches can be reduced to one of the above modes, let us test that statement by analyzing some rows that were formed for compositional purposes unrelated, so far as we know, to any sort of theory about chromatic modes.[4]

Let us choose first an example of an unmixed mode.

Berg's first use of a tone-row occurred in his song, "Schliesse mir die Augen beide mit den Lieben" (second setting, 1925).[5] This row uses the untransposed form of Mode 1 (in our chart).

Example I I0

Schlies - se mir die   Au - gen bei - de   mit den Lie -   ben

The same row is used in the first movement of the *Lyric Suite* (1926).[6]

Example 111

Mode 1.

(G♭   A♭   B♭   D♭   E♭)

The separation of positive and negative tones into two mutually exclusive hexachords means that many diatonic groupings are certain to occur. Combinations of tones from the two hexachords are likely to form recognizable bitonal patterns.

In these works of Berg, the row takes the form of a real theme. As we shall see, subsequent developments of twelve-tone writing lead very far from thematic use.

The next example is more complex, in that it uses a row in which positive and negative tones are mixed. A special compositional aspect of the construction of this row is that the second (complementary) hexachord lies at the fifth above and the fourth below the first hexachord.

Example 112

Schoenberg, *Wind Quintet*, Opus 26

The procedure for analysis is:

a. Examine the tones in Frame 1 assuming that the principal tone is $E\flat$. Any tone that makes a tritone or chromaticism with $E\flat$ or any other note within Frame 1 cannot be part of the positive hexachord; therefore it must be a negative tone belonging to Frame 2. Darken the negative tones in Frame 1.

b. The number of darkened tones in Frame 1 indicates the exchange balance between Frames 1 and 2. Three darkened (negative) tones in Frame 1 means that there will be three undarkened (positive) tones in Frame 2. Darken the remaining negative tones in Frame 2.

Example 113

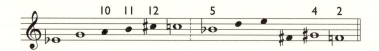

c. Now that the positive tones have been identified, place them in scalewise order in Frame 1; do the same with the negative tones in Frame 2. *D* and *E* have to be lowered an octave to assume the correct scalewise order. Since the tones in Frame 1 indicate Mode 4, the tones in Frame 2 begin with the half-step below the starting note.

Example 114

The pitch content of the above row could be precisely described by saying it is Mode 4, $E\flat$; 10, 11, 12; 5, 4, 2. The Arabic numbers indicate the exchanged pitches, and reveal the extent of the chromaticism in the row (These numbers refer to the position of the tones in the *mode;* not to their positions in the chromatic scale).

Example 115

Si - gno - re,   a - iu - ta- mi   a cam- mi - na - re

Dallapiccola, *Il Prigioniero*[7]

In this case, the row appears as a composed melody with a specific expressive content (prayer).

The first step in finding the mode of this melody is to reduce the pitches in Frame 1 to within an octave of the starting note. The negative notes in Frame 1 need to be identified. These are *D* (tritone against *G♯*), *F* (tritone against *B*), and *G* (chromatic with *B* and *G♯* or *B* and *A♯*). Darken these tones.

Example 116

Reduce the tones of Frame 2 to be within the same octave as those in Frame 1. The exchange is 3–3, so there must be three positive tones in Frame 2. Leaving those notes open, darken the remaining negative tones.

Example 117

Now that the positive and negative tones have been identified, place them in scalewise order within Frames 1 and 2. Since the hexachord in Frame 1 is that of Mode 5, the negative hexachord begins with the half-step below the first note. The concise description of this row is: Mode 5 on *G♯*; 10, 12, 7; 4, 3, 6.

Example 118

The famous row of Berg's *Violin Concerto* contains a number of referential elements. Its odd-numbered notes are the open strings of the violin *(G, D, A, E);* and it has triads, alternately minor and major, on each of these tones (G minor, D major, A minor and E major). With nine tones accounted for, its final three tones complete a tritone group which occurs with the first four notes of the chorale, "Es ist genug," appropriate for the dedication of the piece "To the memory of an Angel" (Manon Gropius, deceased daughter of Alma Mahler).[8]

Example 119

Obviously, much creative compositional thinking went into the formation of this row; and yet it, too, has a well-hidden ancestry among the basic chromatic modes.

Reducing the tones of Frame 1 to scalewise form beginning on G, the pattern reveals only one negative tone, *F♯*. The tones of Frame 2 show only one positive tone, *F*. Placing the two hexachords in their respective frames, the pattern is that of Mode 5 on *G*, with an exchange of 7 and 6. This pattern means a high degree of diatonicism (tonality) in the sonorous result, a characteristic long recognized in this work.

Example 120

Music composed with the twelve tones can assume such a variety of forms, and can be so different in style and content as to leave the mere fact of using twelve tones the only thing held in common between the works. Such is the case if one compares Berg with his fellow Schoenberg pupil, Webern. For Webern, the row became not so much a thematic idea as an organized arrangement of note patterns providing material that could be used to build a form. Schoenberg and Berg used a row to form a theme (in Schoenberg's case, sometimes the other way around); but for Webern, the row itself *became* the theme. Webern, an amateur naturalist, loved to observe how natural objects such as leaves, flowers and crystals grow by the multiplication of similar shapes into larger forms. In that way, the material of Webern's *Concerto*, Opus 24, is generated entirely from two forms of the chromatic formula, *Mm*, a group of three notes bounded by a major third, and containing a minor third and a half-step (see Example 21, derivation of the Eighth Tone, for *Mm* groups 1 and 2).

Calling the *Mm* with its half-step on the bottom No. 1, and the *Mm* with its half-step at the top No. 2, we can see that Webern puts his basic form of the row together with four trichords (a, b, c, and d) using Nos. 1 and 2 alternately.

Example 121

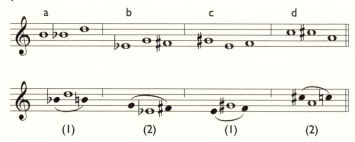

The pitches of Trichord d map into the pitches of a, and the pitches of c map into those of b.

Example 122

A consistent rule of Webern's row is that the melodic interval of a minor third never occurs; the sequence is *B–B♭–D,* or *E♭–G–F♯,* but never *B♭–B–D,* or *E♭–F♯–G.*

The basic row occurs in four forms: (1) the original form; (2) a retrograde form in which each trichord, not the whole row, is read backwards; (3) a form in which the original trichords are alternated, b–a–d–c; and (4) a form which reverses the order of the hexachords, c–d and a–b. Four additional forms are made by the retrogrades of the first four forms.

In all of these forms, the sonorous content is the same, since the same trichords are common to them all. For the purposes of our modal analysis, we need only to consider the first form.

Though the structural implications of this matrix of similarly shaped trichords is paramount over the sonorous element, an analysis of the modal origins of the basic row provides a basis for comparison to other twelve–tone works.

It must be pointed out, however, that if we were able to find its chromatic mode, we would know no more or less about the *Concerto*, Opus 24 than if we were able to ascertain only that a fugue by Bach is in a major key on a certain fundamental pitch.

In finding the negative tones in Frame 1, we see that Trichord a has a negative tone in the middle, and Trichord b has two negative tones with a positive tone in the middle. In Frame 2, the formation is reversed: Trichord c has a positive tone in the middle, and Trichord d has two positive tones with a negative tone in the middle.

The exchange of positive and negative tones is 3–3, evenly laid out so that no two positive or negative tones occur next to each other.

Example 123

The result of such a balanced arrangement of positive and negative tones, sensed if not understood by the listener, is the maximum amount of chromaticism with little reference to diatonicism (tonality). The concise description of this row is: Mode 6 on B; 7, 9, 11; 4, 2, 6.

Example 124

Though all kinds of permutations of two small patterns is the powerful constructional element in this work, it can be no accident that it achieves a negation of tonality, which must have been a pre-compositional intent of Webern's, just as with Berg in the *Lyric Suite* or *Violin Concerto* the intent was to preserve some tonal elements.

Part Two

Practice

Introduction

PART ONE OF THIS BOOK has attempted to establish a general theoretical background for the material of chromatic music—tonal or non-tonal, serial or non-serial. Part Two is intended to be a practical exposition of a method—only one of the many possible ones—of composing with the twelve tones.

The problem for me in formulating this method was to reconcile the powerful cosmology and well-developed procedures of Paul Hindemith with the use of the full chromatic spectrum, which Hindemith's theory had managed to subdue in the interests of tonality, albeit tonality of an expanded kind.

At the same time, I did not want to abandon certain traditional skills in form-building and in the control of sonority which were concomitants of Hindemith's procedures. For example, the method I sought would have to retain the possibility of single-line sketching, a Beethovian process used by Hindemith as the starting point of all his work. Having declared his independence from the major and minor keys, such melodic sketching began with the possibility of choosing *any* tones from the chromatic supply. However, Hindemith's principles of melody (whether the result of theoretical concepts or simply the expression of taste) severely restricted the use of tritones or most overtly chromatic groupings. The result was a kind of melodic line which as a whole might contain all the chromatic tones, but in smaller segments it consisted of diatonic or pentatonic groups which shifted to new areas after a smooth half-step joint between the two areas. Rather than *chromatic,* this sort of melodic structure could better be described as *shifting diatonic.*

In vertical relationships, harmonic or polyphonic, Hindemith's theories (supported by a taste that was probably anti-Wagnerian in origin) apply the same restrictions of tritones and chromaticism. These restrictions led to a large proportion of vertical sonorities that were pentatonic in character, and a certain blandness of harmonic style that characterized Hindemith's music of his middle period, though not earlier or later. Hindemith's ideas of regulating consonance and dissonance *(harmonic fluctuation),* while helpful in controlling undesirable clashes, are not entirely compatible with the intense vocabulary of total chromaticism. Some control can be exercised (the following method attempts to do so), but within a less restrictive framework than the principles stated in the *Craft.*

Once the full chromatic material is available without too many vestigial remnants of tonal procedures, the question still remains as to how to make use of it in compositional processes.

There are basically three kinds of musical construction: monophonic (melody), homophonic (harmony), and polyphonic (polyphony).

The first of these ways of construction—linear use of tone after tone—is the simplest. It has produced many twelve-tone pieces for solo instrument, especially the flute. Pieces that use each tone in successive order, but which distribute the tones among different registers with very few vertical coincidences (many of them by holding some note over while others enter) are still monophonic, even if scored for orchestra.

If serial order itself were to be the guiding principle, that technique can be developed to produce two forms of the same row that fit together making a two-part structure in which upper and lower hexachords have mutually exclusive pitches. However, the selection of such primary rows is complicated, and is an unnecessary pre-compositional step if the main goal is not serial order, but evenly distributed chromaticism.

A two-part structure made by combining rows can also simulate music in more than two parts by *partitioning* segments of the structure. Scoring may produce any texture from chamber ensemble to full orchestra by this method.

The row, originally intended to produce melodic shapes with motivic or thematic significance, can be made to produce chords by lumping three or more tones together. This is a type of homophony, and rather limited in its possibilities since it consumes the pitches at a much more rapid rate than melody; after two six-note chords, the entire row is used. Even further from the original basis of row composition is the construction of chords from the twelve-note supply as a starting point, then using the chord combinations melodically as well as harmonically.

The harmonic method described above has its origins in post-Rameau thinking, in which chords are the building units, and melody consists of arpeggiated chords (as Goetschius once said: "melody grows from chords as branches and leaves grow from a tree trunk").[1]

The third kind of construction, polyphonic, is the one to be utilized here. This approach to the problem of vertical combination is that of the pre-Rameau period: a chord (sonority) is not a pre-existing fixed unit, but a combination of three or more tones, deriving its character from the intervals it contains. The contrapuntal building process is layered, note against note (counterpoint), part against part, which was the prevailing method through at least the first six hundred years of Western music.

In turning to this method of exploiting the chromatic material, it is natural that we adopt some of the pedagogical procedures developed during the polyphonic period. Those procedures were eventually used by J. J. Fux in one of the most influential pedagogical works in the history of theory, *Gradus ad Parnassum* (1725), written after the polyphonic period was over, but all the more useful towards the end of the 18th century as an antidote to the prevailing homophonic style of the time.

This is not the first evocation of Fux in the 20th century, as it occurs significantly in the preface to Hindemith's *Craft*. Hindemith, however, did not utilize the species approach to counterpoint, but developed his own method (which had some medieval precedents) in Volumes II and III of the *Craft*. In this study also, species exercises are not really relevant; but layered construction, as in Hindemith, is to be the building process.

We have already indicated in the discussion above that the main difference between this study and that of Hindemith lies in the full exploitation of chromaticism without the restraining conditions of tonal function; the latter cease to exist for the ear and mind once the positive and negative tones are locked together in a permanent embrace.

Hindemith's cosmology often invokes a Keplerian image of the planetary system, gravity being the force that binds the lesser bodies to the larger. Balanced chromaticism invokes an even larger cosmological image—one of the whole universe in which every positive force is matched by a negative one.

No matter what the method of construction is, the problem of controlling the sonorities remains. This study excludes no possibility, but attempts to develop the technical means needed for the composer to exercise control over the chromatic sonorities—if he does not choose to leave this aspect of his music to accidents of construction or total chance.

∽

6

Tone-sets

DEFINITIONS

W E BEGIN WITH SOME BASIC DEFINITIONS, a few of which
have already been mentioned, but are now
restated in didactic style.

Tone-set. The twelve pitches displayed within one octave, divided into two hexachords and four trichords.

Hexachord 1. The first six pitches, low to high.
Hexachord 2. The second six pitches, low to high.
Trichord a. The first three pitches of Hexachord 1.
Trichord b. The second three pitches of Hexachord 1.
Trichord c. The first three pitches of Hexachord 2.
Trichord d. The second three pitches of Hexachord 2.

Example 125
A Tone-set in primary form.

Matrix. A chart showing the permutations of the trichords.

Each permutation produces a Tone-set which retains the mutual exclusiveness of the hexachords, but varies in the pitch content of the trichords.

The Tone-sets are read by trichord from the top of the chart downwards. For example, Column 1 reads:

$$1\ 2\ 3\ |\ 4\ 5\ 6\ |\ 7\ 8\ 9\ |\ 10\ 11\ 12.$$

Column 6 reads:

$$1\ 3\ 5\ |\ 2\ 4\ 6\ |\ 7\ 9\ 11\ |\ 8\ 10\ 12.$$

Here is the Matrix given in numbers, and applied to the pitches of the Tone-set shown in Example 125 *(see Example 126 on the next page).*

The Matrix retains the hexachordal characteristics of the Tone-set through all the permutations of the trichords, but it offers a continuously unfolding variety of ordering. If one permutation of the Tone-set in the Matrix is followed by another, a ribbon of 120 tones is available for linear construction. Even more variety is available from the patterns in the Matrix, in that the order within each trichord is free. There are six orderings for each trichord. For example, the first trichord of Hexachord 1 could be:

$$1\ 2\ 3\ |\ 1\ 3\ 2\ |\ 2\ 1\ 3\ |\ 2\ 3\ 1\ |\ 3\ 1\ 2\ |\ 3\ 2\ 1.$$

No attempt has been made to expand the Matrix to include all these additional orderings of the trichords. This remains an area of free choice, permitting the composer to choose the tone that best fulfills his melodic, harmonic, or polyphonic intentions.

If the ten permutations of the Tone-sets in the Matrix were utilized in the order shown in the chart, ①, ②, ③, ④, etc., it would be observed that those placed within the double barlines share two of the same pitches in their first trichord (a). To prevent this repetition, a special order of uti-

Example 126

Matrix

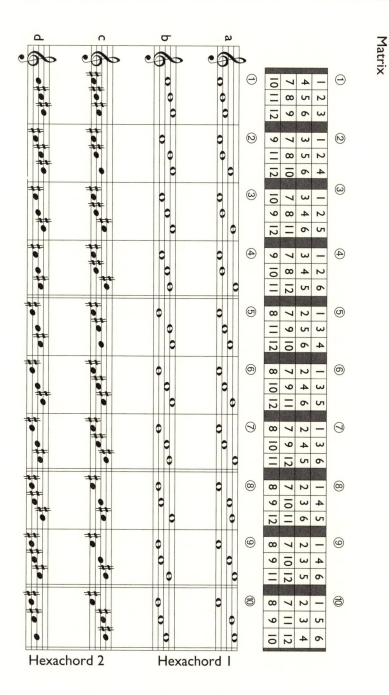

Hexachord 2   Hexachord I

lization is followed that avoids having two of the same pitches of the first trichord of a given permutation duplicated in the first trichord of the succeeding one. The order that accomplishes this objective is:

$$1\ 8\ 4\ 5\ 3\ 7\ 2\ 6\ 9\ (1)\ 10$$
$$1\ 8\ 4\ \text{etc.}$$

To avoid two tones in common, 1 must be inserted between 9 and 10, and repeated after 10 with continuation of the cycle if more tones are needed.

The above sequence of numbers, which originates from a purely musical objective, is not numerically as unorganized as it might appear. It follows progressive rules which place the numbers in pairs that add up to the final number of a series (nine, in this case). Similar rules can be applied to form such sequences between the number 1 and any odd number. The following diagram shows the pattern of the sequence given here.

Example 127

USE OF THE MATRIX IN
MELODIC CONSTRUCTION

The long ribbon of tones provided by the Matrix assures as low an incidence of recurring tones as possible. It is to be regarded as totally unrelated to the formal syntax. There is no reason to relate the completion of a Tone-set to the length of a phrase. The latter springs from a rhythmical impulse, or in a text setting, from the length of the poetic phrase. Just as a ribbon or a bolt of cloth is cut at the point necessary for the shape of the garment, so is the ribbon of tones from the

Matrix cut at any point. Tones do not have to be jammed into too small a space in order to arrive at the end of a Tone-set.

It may be tempting to treat the first note of the primary set as a *tonic*. This concept does not work, necessarily, because any one of the three tones in the first trichord may be used first.

Similarly, there is no reason to continue the ending merely to reach a particular tone to simulate a tonal ending, though this procedure is possible if desired. In music which is not tonally oriented there are many devices that can suggest closure other than stopping on a note which is prominent at the beginning.

The following examples will show how melodic phrase construction proceeds without regard to the segmentations of the Matrix.

Examples 128 and 129 are main themes at the start of instrumental works. Both of them use the regular sequence of the trichords without repetitions.

Example 128

Example 129

Repetition of tones is not necessarily excluded; direct repetition, or a return to a previously used tone within the
trichord may occur. Also, one or two tones of a given trichord
may reappear after the beginning of the succeeding trichord.

The rate at which new pitches are introduced (speed of unfolding) is a compositional decision not to be forced by the
mere availability of the pitches provided by the Matrix.

In the following examples, repetition expands most of the
trichords beyond a simple exposition of the three tones. Example 130 is from a song with piano. Example 131 is an aria
with flute obbligato. The melody of the flute uses the same
Tone-set as the vocal line; however each form of the melody
is adapted to its medium, with resulting differences in the
durations of the tones, range, and melodic curve.

Example 130

Example 131

The soft — com-plain - ing flute In dy - ing notes dis - cov-ers the woes of hope - less lov - ers, whose dirge is whisp - ered by the warb - ling lute. —

GENERATION OF TONE-SETS FROM TRICHORDS

It is immediately evident in the above examples that the Tone-set itself does not generate the *musical* idea. There is nothing motivic in the Tone-sets, unless one wishes to call the triad grouping of Example 130 a motive.

The Tone-set is only raw material, such as a piece of wood or stone that a sculptor may shape into an art object. Nevertheless, the raw material has characteristics of its own before and above what the artist does to it. Let us examine some of the properties of various Tone-sets.

We have seen that chromatic material is on another level of complexity compared to the simpler pentatonic or diatonic orders. However, as in all kinds of evolution, characteristics of the simpler species are not necessarily annihilated, but are absorbed into the more advanced ones (*symbiosis,* as it is called in biology). Human cells have characteristics deriving from the simplest forms of life; human bodies retain remnants from every stage on the way to *homo sapiens.*

Every Tone-set, by the same symbiotic process, contains intervals and tone-groups from the simpler pentatonic and diatonic orders along with the more complex chromatic patterns.

Schoenberg once put forth the above view of musical development when he expressed to Winfried Zillig[1] the hope that future music theory might treat tonality (diatonicism) as a special case of twelve-tone music (chromaticism). This view implies that tonality is not destroyed by chromaticism, but absorbed within it.

Trichords reveal their ancestry by their interval groupings. Some contain groups which may occur in pentatonic music (no half-step, tritone or chromatic formula). Some may contain groups which cannot occur in pentatonic music (half-step or tritone), but are not chromatic, therefore diatonic. And finally, some contain groups which can occur only in a chromatic context (chromatic formulas).

Since the Matrix offers a condensed picture of the pitch structure which will result from the use of a given Tone-set in composition, the balance it reveals between pentatonic, diatonic and chromatic trichords will relate to that of the whole work. Just as a classical composer used to be able to direct the broadest aspect of the sound-structure of his work by choosing a major or minor mode, one can now exert a precompositional influence on a chromatic work by the choice of a particular Tone-set.

It has been pointed out that Tone-sets can be generated from chromatic modes by the exchange of positive and negative tones. This is one way of starting, but here we will examine the results of these tone combinations in more "humanistic" terms. It will not be enough to describe them by formulas such as "Mode 5 on G♯, 10–12–7, 4–3–6" (Part One, Examples 115–118, Dallapiccola). This precise description would enable us to write out the Tone-set, but it would tell nothing about its musical characteristics. We would know more about its effect if we were to describe the trichords in terms of their ancestry from the larger divisions of tonal material: pentatonic, diatonic and chromatic. These divisions have cultural and historical resonances, along with the objective fact that they give us a gradation from simple (vibration ratios) to complex.

The Dallapiccola Tone-set regarded in this manner, could be described as follows:

> Trichord a—diatonic, minor.
> Trichord b—pentatonic.
> Trichord c—chromatic.
> Trichord d—diatonic, Phrygian.

The hexachords are both chromatic, which can demonstrated by extracting the formulas contained in them. These are:

Example 132

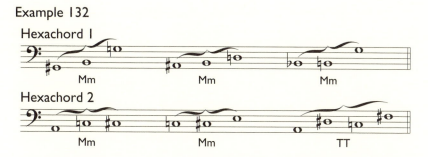

Hexachord 1

Hexachord 2

In the Tone-sets which follow here, the approach to construction (this need not be the only one) is to begin with the trichords as musical entities, rather than to construct the Tone-sets from the chromatic modes by interchanging tones.

Of great importance in determining the character of a Tone-set (and the kind of music that will result from its use) is the first trichord, simply because of its advantageous position. Therefore, the first pre-compositional decision has to do with these three notes. Should the first trichord be a simple pattern (i. e., non-chromatic) or a complex one (chromatic)?

Once the pattern of the first Trichord a is decided, Trichord b is added, but its individual character is not the main consideration; that consideration is now the overall quality of the hexachord that is formed (Hexachord 1).

The completion of Hexachord 1 is as far as decision-making may go; Hexachord 2 is already determined, since it consists of the remaining (complementary) pitches. However, Trichords c and d must be analyzed in the same way as Trichords a and b, since their contribution to the whole Matrix is equally important. Should the analysis of Trichords c and d show undesired results as far as the whole contents of the Tone-set is concerned (e. g., too much or too little chromaticism), the only solution is to alter one or the other of the two hexachords until the desired balance is achieved.

The following examples will illustrate the formation of Tone-sets.

Example 133a

If Trichord a is pentatonic, Trichord b, since it adds a sixth tone, must make Hexachord 1 at least diatonic.

Example 133b

If a chromatic relationship occurs between Trichords a and b, Hexachord 1 must be chromatic, though it is a combination of two pentatonic trichords.

Example 133c

If Trichord a is diatonic, Trichord b may avoid adding chromaticism, thereby leaving Hexachord 1 diatonic.

Example 133d

Trichord b may be pentatonic, but if Trichord a is diatonic, the entire hexachord is diatonic; a hexachord may not be classified lower than its most complex component.

Example 133e

If Trichord a is chromatic, the entire hexachord is chromatic,

Example 133f

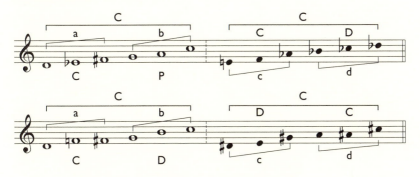

even if Trichord b is pentatonic, or diatonic.

ANALYSIS OF TONE-SETS

Now that we have established the framework for constructing a Tone-set taking into account the trichordal content, let us apply the terminology to the reverse process, analyzing the trichordal content of Example 125 (for which Example 126 is the matrix), and Examples 128 through 137, for which we do not need to give the Matrixes here. Of the forty trichords each Matrix yields, the profile according to pentatonic, diatonic and chromatic is as follows:

	Pentatonic	Diatonic	Chromatic
Example 125	37	7	0
Example 128	20	16	4
Example 129	14	22	4
Example 130	15	12	13
Example 131	1	27	12

The differences in these profiles show how much variety there can be in Tone-sets using the twelve chromatic tones. Each of these profiles has a distinct character that will manifest itself in the melodic line, and, as we shall see later, through all the vertical and oblique combinations of the tones, as long as the integrity of the established hexachordal order is maintained.

☙

7

Two-Part Polyphony

INTRODUCTION

TONE-SETS AS WE HAVE SEEN THEM ABOVE provide a rich material for melodic construction—far more than modal or major and minor scales, or even the seventy-two *melas* or *thatas* of Indian music. If our Western music were to regress from the polyphonic concept that is its special genius, an organized theory for melodic construction would suffice, in the same way diatonic modes did from antiquity until the beginning of polyphony, around the tenth century. At that time, after a period of thickening monodic sound by coupling voices at the octave, fifth or fourth in parallel motion, Western polyphony took its first steps in freeing the motion of the added voice from the principal melody by procedures which resulted in differences of direction between the two voices. The added voice would stand still while the principal voice moved up or down (oblique motion); or when the principal voice moved in one direction, the added voice moved the other way (contrary motion).

As for the tone supply, both the principal voice and the added voice drew from the same source: the mode of the existing melody, or in a more general way, from the range of diatonic tones (later called *gamut*) inherited from the Greeks

147

and proven by derivation on the monochord.

If two voices are drawing on the same tone source, and it is limited to seven pitches, the circumstance that they draw the same tone (resulting in an octave or unison) must be limited if diversity of the voices is to be maintained. In a unison, one tone literally swallows the other, and the octave does so almost to the same degree. The interval of the fifth, next in concordance to the octave, also needs some restrictions if diversity of sound as well as direction is to be assured.

In general one could say that the objective of the "rules" of polyphony, as they evolved, was to achieve diversity of the component parts along with the avoidance of intervals which combined too well or clashed too harshly. The earliest polyphony gave priority to the perfect consonances. Later practice included the imperfect consonances but excluded all dissonances except under conditions in which melodic function softened their harshness.

If we were to seek the same general objective in chromatic polyphony using Tone-sets instead of modes or scales, we would have to follow certain guide-lines to achieve the desired result.

The first difference between the old and the new polyphony arises from the great increase in the tone supply—a pool of twelve pitches instead of seven. We have observed that twelve-tone music is more sensitive to tone repetition than pentatonic or diatonic music. The very nature of chromatic music establishes the principle of maximum pitch change. Another part added to the principal part, then, must not bring the same pitches close to their appearance in the principal part, since that would be simply repetition in a different register.

With the above problem, we are helped by the hexachordal construction of the Tone-sets. If only the tones of Hexachord 2 are used in the part added to Hexachord 1, and vice versa, there can be no unisons or octaves.

The pattern of the hexachords and trichords would appear as follows:

Example 134

	Hexachord 1		Hexachord 2	
Principal Voice	a	b	c	d
Added Voice	c	d	a	b
	Hexachord 2		Hexachord 1	

THE TREATMENT OF INTERVALS

In the treatment of intervals formed between the parts, the octave is automatically ruled out; it cannot occur between the tones of mutually exclusive hexachords. However, we must establish "rules" for the use of other intervals.

The fifth, standing alone in a chromatic context, is like a fish out of water; it produces a consonant hole in the texture which otherwise maintains a certain tension. Also, the strength of its root tends to unbalance the floating nature of this polyphony. Therefore, in two-part counterpoint the fifth is to be avoided. If more parts are to be added later, and the lower note of a fifth is the lowest note of the whole complex, it may produce a chord with a strong root which could be intrusive in the flow of chromatic harmony.

At the other end of the spectrum, towards the dissonant side, minor seconds and minor ninths in two-part polyphony produce the harshest clashes. One such interval is conspicuous and may be unbalancing; several in succession (even with sufficient contrary motion) begin to suggest that there is no polyphony at all, but merely an added part which has somehow gotten out of phase with the principle part.

The demotion of fifths and minor seconds or ninths leaves thirds and sixths, minor and major sevenths; and the fourth, major ninth, and tritone as the unrestricted intervals in two-part polyphony.

Independence of the parts has always been promoted (as far as the spatial aspect is concerned) by contrary motion, defaulted by oblique motion, and lost by similar motion—especially by leaps in similar motion. These priorities need to be kept in mind in chromatic counterpoint as well as in any kind of independent polyphony.

CANTUS FIRMUS

In order to experience some of the possibilities inherent in chromatic polyphony based on Tone-sets, we shall use a type of exercise long familiar in music theory: a short *cantus firmus* to which note-against-note counterpoint is added. The cantus firmus of traditional studies was not necessarily a known chant melody, but often an invented row of tones in one of the modes. In this case, the cantus firmus will be a twelve-tone melodic structure made from a Tone-set.

Whereas the traditional cantus firmus comes to a closed ending on the note with which it began, these rows do not; they represent only a segment of what could be an ongoing structure.

The Tone-sets previously given in Example 133 are not "melodic" structures because they merely follow a fixed order from low to high. They become melodic when the order of their notes and some of their octave positions are varied, when a melodic "shape" is created which has contours that are not completely predictable, and when step-wise motion is varied by interval leaps. Although the tonal content is the same as in the Tone-set, the attention is directed to intervals formed by the leaps, and to linear (i. e., step-wise) relationships between some non-adjacent tones (step-progression, as Hindemith calls it).[1]

There can be no prescription for introducing order change, leaps or step-progressions into a melodic line, but these are the occurrences which make the difference between a mere tone succession, such as a scale or Tone-set, and a "melody."

For the purposes of these cantus firmus melodies, changes of register do not exceed an octave, and interval leaps do not exceed a seventh.

Here below are melodic lines based on the Tone-sets of Example 133. The analysis was done *after* the melodies were formed. Musical impulse (as vague as that may seem) must come into play in forming melodies, even at this level. One cannot arbitrarily insert an order change, octave transposition or step-progression. These events come about in shaping the line, in which the feeling for contour plays a part as it does when an artist draws a line.

Example 135

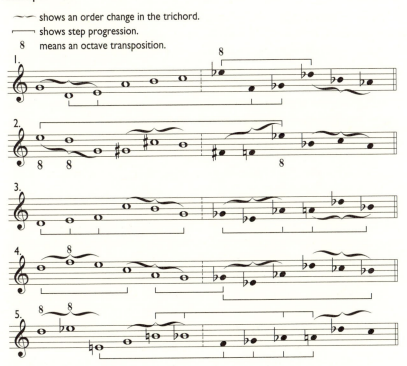

Example 135 (continued)

THE COMPLEMENTARY VOICE

An added part formed from the complementary tones cannot be as free melodically as the principal voice (this is equally true in tonal music). Though the trichord content is pre-ordained by the complementary relationship, the melodic shape has to be arranged to satisfy two conditions:

1. The spatial relationship ought to show independence of the principal voice according to the priorities stated above: contrary motion is preferred, and similar motion is possible except when both parts leap (applicable only in two-part counterpoint).

2. The intervals between the parts should be regulated according to the priorities described above. Fifths and minor seconds or ninths are to be avoided (again, the restriction on the fifth is applicable only in two-part counterpoint). If an impasse occurs as a result of trying to meet the above conditions, there is an "escape clause": one tone of a trichord in the complementary voice may be omitted and one tone held over, resulting

in oblique motion. Omitted tones are noted (circled) below the second voice. The omission of one pitch in the added part does no harm to the chromatic context as a whole since it is already complete in the principal voice. However, in these exercises no tone of a trichord should be omitted unless there is no satisfactory alternative.

Here are the cantus firmus melodies of Example 135 with added complementary voices to illustrate the principles described above.

Example 136

8

Three-Part Polyphony

THE THIRD VOICE

IF WE WISH TO ADD A THIRD VOICE, *3v*, to the principal voice, *Pv* and the complementary voice, *Cv*, we now have to use the existing trichords in different positions. For example:

Example 137

Pv	a	b	c	d
3v	d	a	b	c
Cv	c	d	a	b

or

Pv	a	b	c	d
3v	d	c	b	a
Cv	c	d	a	b

The melodic line formed in *3v* is hardly that; the conditions to be met in finding the best placement of the tones are such that the linear element is the last thing to be considered. The situation is similar to that of a contratenor (usually instrumental) added to the tenor and motetus in the polyphony of the fourteenth century: its purpose was to add the note needed for a complete triad wherever possible.[1] Consequently, a contratenor moved from between to above or be-

155

low the two existing parts with little regard for its own melodic line.

The *3v* in the examples which follow do not cross over the *Pv* or *Cv*. Also, its line should avoid wide intervals as much as possible. The space it uses may lie close to that of the related trichord (i. e., the one in the same hexachord): d added to c would probably lie in the bass clef; b added to c would probably lie in the treble clef. The *3v* can, if necessary, be written partly in one clef and partly in the other.

CONTRAPUNTAL RELATIONS

As for contrapuntal motion, the *3v* may go in the same direction as one of the existing parts if they themselves are moving in contrary motion; or if the existing voices are moving in the same direction, the *3v* should go in contrary motion to one of them.

The above procedure seeks to achieve as much independence as possible between the voices. If in any case all three voices must move in the same direction, at least one voice must move stepwise. Allowing all three voices to leap in the same direction negates the independence of all three.

As for interval relationships, the *3v* in these exercises should avoid the restricted minor second or minor ninth with the voice above or below. A fifth should not be formed with the lowest voice, but may occur with the voice above.

Octaves, of course, cannot occur between the tones of different trichords, but "false relation of the octave" can occur if the same tone used at the end of one trichord is used at the beginning of its occurrence in the voice above or below (this is at the point where the trichords change places). The internal order of the trichords needs to be arranged to avoid such octave cross relations. The following example illustrates the places at which such problems may occur.

Example 138

Pv	a	b	c	d
3v	d	c	b	a
Cv	c	d	a	b

Pv	a	b	c	d
3v	b	a	d	c
Cv	c	d	a	b

DISSONANCE LEVEL

To maintain tension above the triad level, one should attempt to have each three-part sonority contain at least one dissonant interval (except the minor second or minor ninth). In this style, it is also desirable to have a tritone or chromaticism in each sonority whenever possible. If no solution prevents a major or minor triad from occurring, at least it will not occur in its $\frac{5}{3}$ form because of the restriction of the interval a fifth above the lowest part. Of the other forms of the triad, the $\frac{6}{4}$ is preferred because its instability fits in better with the dissonant sonorities.

Within the general dissonance level established, there will always be "fluctuation" (Hindemith's term).[2] As in triadic polyphony, there are differences between those triads which, according to the mode or scale used, have different interval structures. These forms of the triad are normally taken as they come in the flow of polyphony, without any attempt to specifically regulate the fluctuation of tension. With the style defined here, there is also a general level within which variations may occur. It is equally impossible (as with triadic polyphony) to strictly control the tension of individual sonorities. Such a process is workable only in an harmonic approach which treats chords as individual blocks, not as the result of moving lines.

To summarize, the addition of the *3v* has to be accomplished with the following objectives in mind:

1. Avoidance of undesired octave cross relations with either part.
2. Independent spatial movement; all three parts should rarely go in the same direction.
3. Keeping the dissonance threshold at the same level as in the original two-voice structure (no minor seconds or minor ninths between any of the voices).
4. Formation of as reasonable a melodic line as possible under the above conditions, staying within the space permitted by the two existing voices.

To illustrate the process of choosing the notes for the third voice, the following illustration, based on Example 136-2, shows all permutations of each added trichord. One has to go through these possibilities in choosing the best solution, though it is not always necessary to write them down. The one marked *best* has acceptable intervals combined with the most independent voice-leading.

Example 139

x = m2 or m9   o = fifth against the bass   un = unison   tr = triad

Example 139 (continued)

NOTATION PROBLEMS

These exercises bring to the fore the problem inherent in using our conventional notation (evolved for diatonic music) for chromatic music. Having been constructed layer by layer, the spelling of each trichord in this case adheres to that which it had in the original Tone-set. This policy helps in understanding the construction, but leads to very strange chromatic spellings of simple diatonic or pentatonic three-note sonorities. No attempt is made to re-spell them here; this might in fact lead to equally bad spellings of the individual lines. Of course, in free chromatic writing, the best policy is to achieve the simplest readability, changing sharps or flats at any time, regardless of the spelling in the original Tone-set. Also, any number of redundant accidentals is permissible if necessary for clarity and security in reading. One thing to be learned from this study, aside from the principles of chromatic counterpoint, is to accept the absolute equality and interchangeability of the spellings of every tone—one of the inevitable consequences of equal temperament.

Here below are the two-voice structures of Example 136 with an added voice, *3v,* worked out according the two possible formats (d–c–b–a, or b–a–d–c).

After completion, the sonorities are analyzed according to the symbols given earlier (Chapter 4). At a glance, one can see to what extent tritonic or chromatic, or dissonant second/seventh tension is maintained and where it increases or lessens.

Example 140a

Example 140a (continued)

Figure 140b

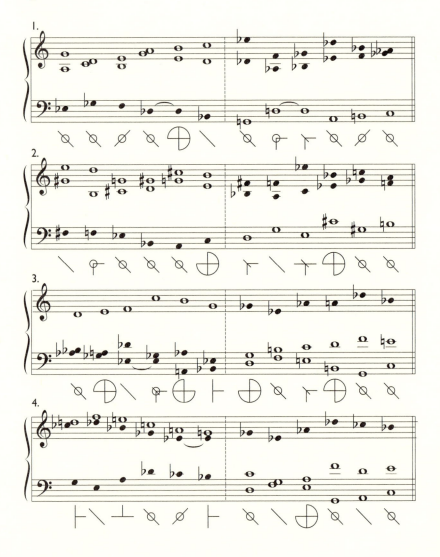

Example 140b (continued)

9

Four-Part Polyphony

THE FOURTH VOICE

T HE ADDITION OF A FOURTH VOICE *(4v)* to the three-voiced exercises above extends the system of trichordal relationships to its maximum. The added trichords must be the ones not already present above or below, indicated in the following diagram by an arrow.

Example 141

Pv	a	b	c	d
→ 4v	b	a	d	c
3v	d	c	b	a
Cv	c	d	a	b

Pv	a	b	c	d
3v	b	a	d	c
→ 4v	d	c	b	a
Cv	c	d	a	b

The spacing of the three-voiced examples must be opened up to permit the addition of the *4v*. The *Pv* should be transposed up an octave.

164

If the alignment of the three-voiced example is a d c, the *4v* (b) is inserted between a and d.

These examples have almost nothing in common with traditional four-voiced choral texture; they had best be thought of as for string quartet, with no range limitations other than those.

Spacing for the harmonies, since there are no doublings, needs to be wide. Because the lowest part has no strong root function, it does not need to be kept far from the upper voices, nor do the upper voices need to be closer together.

The melodic quality of the *4v* is pushed even further to the background than that of the *3v;* it has such obstacles to overcome in fulfilling its harmonic function that any melodic shape is satisfactory if it accomplishes the goal of a good sonority within the established limits of dissonance.

The previous "escape clause" must sometimes be evoked with the *4v,* and extended even further. Besides using a tie and omitting one trichord tone, there may now be two adjoining ties, omitting two trichords tones. Also, a note may be repeated after one intervening tone. These flexibilities make it possible to control the dissonance level within the previous limits. Here below are the three-voiced structures of Example 140 with a *4v* added.

Example 142a

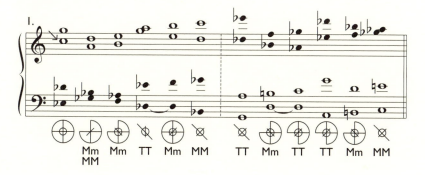

Example 142a (continued)

Example 142a (continued)

Example 142b

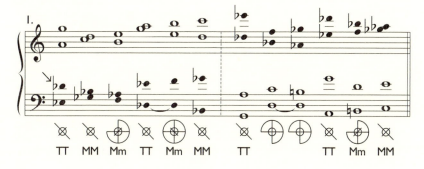

Example 142b (continued)

Example 142b (continued)

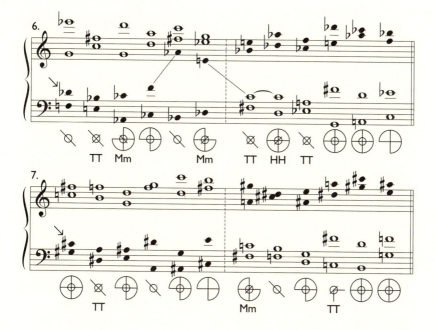

10

The Dissonant Style

THE DISSONANT STYLE

THE EXERCISES IN EXAMPLES 136–142 define a style, one which we may call *consonant-chromatic,* since it restricts the harshest clashes. The discipline gained from working within these restrictions makes it possible to form the basis for its opposite, a style we could define as *dissonant-chromatic.*

In the dissonant-chromatic style, two-voiced counterpoint seeks to use the *m2* or *m9* wherever possible. Next in favor would be the *M7, M2, m7,* and *T.* Sixths, thirds, and the perfect fourth fall into the least favored group. The fifth, as before, is excluded completely.

If some of the least favored intervals occur by necessity in the two-voiced counterpoint, it is possible to offset them by dissonances when a third voice is added. If the three-voiced structure lacks enough dissonance, the fourth voice may supply it.

In chromatic polyphony, there will be great differences of effect between one sonority and another, even when the general guidelines for the consonant or dissonant style are followed. Control of dissonance is general and not always specific for individual sonorities, although for expressive pur-

170

poses (as is the case in tonal music) a specific sonority can be made to stand out. The variety that follows from the flow of polyphonic choices adds a certain element of unpredictability within the established controls—not an undesirable result. However, this does not mean that anything that comes first should be accepted as "in the flow of the polyphony." The possibilities for varying arrangements of the tones in the trichords should be sorted out for the best possible result available within the intended stylistic level.

The following examples (Example 143) show melodies 3 and 7 from Example 135 set in dissonant chromatic style, first in a two-part setting (those from Example 136 cannot be reused here), and then with the addition of the *3v* and *4v*.

The resulting three- and four-voiced sonorities are again analyzed by symbols. An examination of the symbols will show that the three-voiced settings do not always maintain tritonic or chromatic tension; three notes can be chromatic only if all of them belong to one chromatic formula. In a few cases, not even a *m2* or *M7* is possible, but any form of consonant triad is avoided.

The four-voiced settings are naturally more successful in maintaining dissonance. No. 3, which has a diatonic first hexachord, manages to produce a four-voice setting consisting almost entirely of sonorities containing chromaticism, and all twelve sonorities have a *m2* or *M7* dissonance. No. 7, which has more chromaticism in its melody, produces only three chromatic sonorities, and three in which *M2* and *m7* dissonances are the sharpest intervals. Whereas No. 3 contains some sonorities with chromaticism but no tritone, every one of the twelve sonorities of No. 7 contains a tritone.

One can see from the above statistics how each Tone-set, when developed through melody and counterpoint, produces its own group of sonorities, and these will account for the sonorous flavor of any musical structure built upon that particular Tone-set.

Example 143

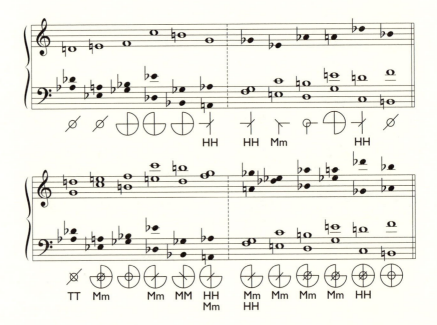

Example 143 (continued)

11

Polyphony With More or Less
Than Note-Against-Note

POLYPHONY WITH MORE OR LESS
THAN NOTE-AGAINST-NOTE

ALL OF THE PREVIOUS POLYPHONIC EXAMPLES have been in note-against-note counterpoint. A traditional method of contrapuntal training begins with note-against-note writing, then introduces counterpoint with more than one note against the other ("florid counterpoint"). Some of the additional notes in these exercises are given special treatment because they form dissonances according to the established norm of the period. The dissonances are treated as ornamental rather than fundamental pitches. In chromatic counterpoint, none of the notes are purely ornamental, though in free rhythm some notes may gain prominence over others through length or favorable metric placement. In chromatic counterpoint, diversity of rhythm between the parts is not normally the result of additional subsidiary notes (though such a thing is possible) but is the result of varying speeds of unfolding the twelve notes in different voices.

The problem in having various speeds of pitch-unfolding is that the mutual exclusiveness of the hexachords of the original Tone-set has to be preserved. The slower or faster unfolding voice cannot fall back or move ahead to the extent that its pitches come together with the same ones in another voice, producing octave cross relations.

In free composition, the *Cv* may include only a few notes selected from those available in the Matrix; or as many notes as the *Pv,* with the full status of a complementary theme; or, by means of repetition, more notes than the *Pv.*

If fewer notes are needed in the *Cv* than in the *Pv,* some pitches must be omitted. This does no damage to the overall chromaticism, since all of the twelve pitches are already present in the *Pv.*

If rhythmical or thematic reasons should require *more* notes in the *Cv* than in the *Pv,* tone repetition must be used to prevent the *Cv* (Hexachord 2) from advancing into the same pitch area as the *Pv* (Hexachord 1).

We can experience some of the problems of chromatic counterpoint other than note-against-note by exercises similar to those of species counterpoint, though still in unmeasured notes.

In the examples below, the restrictions of consonant-chromatic counterpoint are observed: no minor seconds, minor ninths or fifths between the *Cv* and the *Pv.* The rule applies in full force at the point where the two voices fall together. The intervening tones of the faster moving part may, if necessary, form restricted intervals.

The following examples, without meter, illustrate some alignments of two voices other than note-against-note.

    a. Two notes in the *Cv* placed against three in the *Pv* (one note in each trichord of the of the *Cv* is omitted.

Example 144a

(E♭) (A♭) (D) (A)

b. One note in the *Cv* against three in the *Pv* (two notes of each trichord in the *Cv* are omitted).

Example 144b

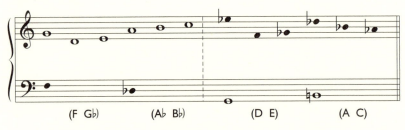

(F G♭) (A♭ B♭) (D E) (A C)

c. Two notes in the *Cv* against each note of the *Pv* (Hexachord 2 unfolds twice under Hexachord 1).

Example 144c

d. Three notes in the Cv against each note of the Pv (Hexachord 2 unfolds three times against Hexachord 1).

Example 144d

In Examples e, f, g, and h, the alignments are the same as in a, b, c, and d, but the *Pv* is the lower voice.

Example 144e

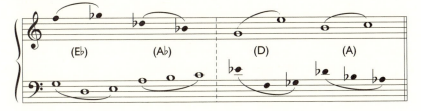

Example 144f

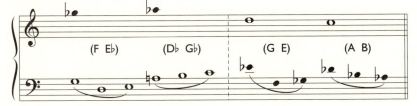

Example 144g

Example 144h

Part Three

Examples from Compositions

Examples from Compositions

THE EXAMPLES IN THE PREVIOUS CHAPTER, which place a certain number of notes against others, are as far removed from real music as the florid exercises of species counterpoint. At this stage, we need the varied rhythmic environment of actual music to see how the trichords may unfold at different rates, and how the problems of pitch distribution may be handled to maintain a consistent chromatic flow.

Example 145 is from a string quartet. The analysis begins in the middle of the bar after letter N. The *Pv* unfolds rapidly in triplets. Two other parts accompany it to support the meter on the first note of each triplet. These parts take their notes from the complementary trichord, omitting unneeded notes in each case. The notes of the complementary trichord are shaded, and the letter names of the omitted notes are bracketed.

For this example, the complete Matrix is given. The trichords in columns ③, ⑦, ②, and ⑥ are applicable.

Example 145a

181

Example 145b

Example 145c

Example 146, from a symphony, shows statements of the *Pv,* a passacaglia theme in which the twelve pitches assume different orders (following the Matrix) on each statement. The Tone-set is:

Example 146a

In the first of the statements shown here, the theme is played by the violas, and a bassoon plays a countermelody below it which unfolds three trichords against one: b, c, d against a; a, c, d against b; a, b, d against c, and a, b, c against d. The trichords are in permutation ⑧, as follows:

Example 146b

The next statement, again with the theme in the violas, has a clarinet obbligato following the same distribution pattern, but with different pitches since the trichords are in permutation ④.

Example 146c

The third statement in this example has the theme given by a solo trumpet, with a canon at the octave both below and above it played by woodwinds. The trichord permutation is ⑤.

Example 146d

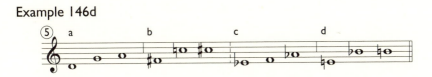

Example 146e

The musical examples shown so far in this chapter have been contrapuntal in texture. It is true that the additive method of construction lends itself well to contrapuntal structures. But just as block harmonic construction broken up by scalar and arpeggiated figurations can be developed into contrapuntal textures (though it is more adaptable to homophony), the additive method can develop homophonic textures expressed as chords, arpeggiation and running figures (though it is more adaptable to polyphony).

Example 147, from a song, shows a chordal accompaniment to the vocal line, though the chords are formed contrapuntally by combinations of tones from the trichords of the Matrix.

Example 147

Example 148 is from a song that was composed beginning not with the melodic line (as is the case with other examples shown here) but with block harmonies derived from the matrix.

Each harmony has six tones (plus one doubled note) of a given permutation, sounded several times as required by a rhythmic sketch of the text. The harmonies are arpeggiated downwards ("Flowing sheets of rain"), and other single tones in the right hand support the pitches of the vocal melody.

The vocal melody is formed from tones other than those in the arpeggio at the same time. For example, if the arpeggio is using the trichords a and c, the vocal melody uses tones from b and d. Or if the arpeggio uses a and c, the vocal melody uses d and b.

Example 148

1. Flowing Sheets of Rain

The sort of motion which in tonal music is made by short arpeggiations or scale figures can be developed equally well from trichord patterns. Examples 149 and 150 illustrate this process. Example 149 takes its clue from the words "phrase upon phrase of endless thought patterns." The accompaniment is an endless succession of trichord patterns.

In this case, the vocal line was composed first. The accompaniment uses no tone present at the same time in the vocal line (no "cross relations of the octave"). However, the rapid motion, played softly and usually not in the same octave as the vocal line, causes no trouble for the singer with a secure sense of melodic intervals.

Example 149 has the same Tone-set as Example 148.

Example 149

5. Thought Patterns

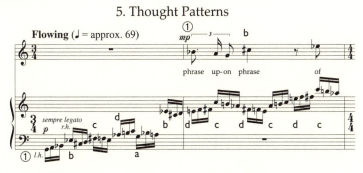

Example 150 has a continuous motion accompaniment that supports the pitches of the vocal line by using the tones of the same trichord in the right hand. The contrary tones are in the bass, far enough away so that they do not disturb the singer.

Example 150a

Example 150b

brought me rings,——— he gave me songs,——— he was——— the

The examples shown so far in this chapter, whether homophonic or polyphonic, have not contained vertical structures of more than four pitches. The highest chromatic density can be achieved by the interplay of all four trichords: the twelve tones can be evenly distributed in all dimensions when the integrity of the trichords and hexachords is maintained.

Example 151

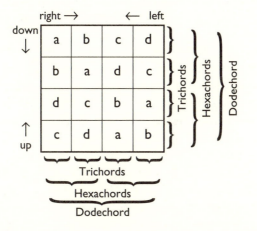

The pleasing balance of the above diagram does not mean that four-voiced texture is a necessary limit for chromatic music; no composer would submit to a principle that confined him to sonorities containing no more than four different pitches. Yet, vertical groupings of more than four pitches quickly expend the energy capital given by pitch-change. It is possible to have two five-note sonorities that do not duplicate any pitch between them. But the third such sonority can introduce only two pitches not already heard. After that, every pitch must have been used shortly before. Change of register is useful in disguising repetitions, but it does not provide the freshness of new pitches. With the six-note sonority, only one other such sonority can be used before pitch repetition begins. One of the forms of musical energy—pitch change—is exhausted after the six-note level; all that remains is the addition of further dissonances until the "white noise" (or "black hole") of the all-pitch, twelve-note sonority is reached. Continuous dissonance beyond the level of controlled pitch-change can only function in situations where elements other than pitch have taken the upper hand—not an uncommon occurrence in twentieth century music.

Far short of such extremes, there are compositional situations in which a large dissonant sonority may be needed. There can be no rules for such cases—each sonority has to be developed *ad hoc;* but preventing the duplication of pitches in the immediately preceding or succeeding sonority will enhance the effectiveness of the large sonority.

In Example 152, again from a song, the excerpt starts at a point where permutation ② of the Matrix is in use. The vocal part expresses the trichords c and d. The accompaniment in the first measure gives another illustration of four-voiced harmony made from the polyphonic combination of the four trichords. The Pv uses c (to support the pitches of the vocal line), the Cv is b; d and a are the $3v$ and $4v$. On the fourth beat of the second measure, a fifth tone enters. In the third measure, a sixth and seventh tone are added, and two of these change on the second quarter-note. None of these tones double the $F\sharp$ (from d) held by the vocal part. In the third bar, ten different pitches are used; eight remain in the final sonority. The two pitches not used are A and C; both would have resulted in minor seconds which would have clouded the sonority more than was desired.

Example 152a

Example 152b

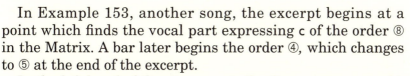

In Example 153, another song, the excerpt begins at a point which finds the vocal part expressing c of the order ⑧ in the Matrix. A bar later begins the order ④, which changes to ⑤ at the end of the excerpt.

In the left hand of the piano part, the *Cv* expresses a and b against c and d of the vocal part; a is expressed linearly, and b is a chord. The right hand forms an eighth-note accompaniment figure to support the voice from the tones of c and d. At the beginning of ④, the eighth-note motion in the accompaniment ceases. As the vocal part expresses b, c, and d, the accompaniment uses large chords with six or seven notes. The upper notes support the vocal part, and the lower notes form the complements: a, c, and d (against b); b, d and a (against c); and c, a and b (against d).

In the last bar of the excerpt, six-note chords are formed from the combination of two trichords in regular order (not crossed over as in the previous sonorities).

Example 153a

Example 153b

Example 154, from a symphony, shows how the presence of all four trichords may intensify a high point in a melodic phrase. The excerpt shows the melody in permutation ⑤ of the Matrix for three bars, changing to permutation ⑥ for the remaining bars.

In the first bar, the bass line (cellos and basses) has c and d against a and b in the melody (violins). An inner part (violas) has b and a. At the second bar, the melody reaches its

high point in *crescendo*. The violins are joined by the violas
and flutes, and bassoons double the cellos and basses.

There are now two main lines (*Pv* and *Cv*) expressing c
and d in the top part and a and d in the lower. Oboes, clari-
nets, horns and trumpets (at the $\frac{2}{4}$ bar) fill the space in the
middle of the texture with tones of the trichords *not* present
in the outer lines. This means that all four trichords are expressed within each measure (several omitted tones are
shown encircled). In the fourth bar, permutation ⑥ begins in
all parts with the same alignment.

The excerpt is shown in full score and in reduction from
the $\frac{2}{4}$ bar to the end.

Example 154a

Example 154b

Example 154b (continued)

Example 154c

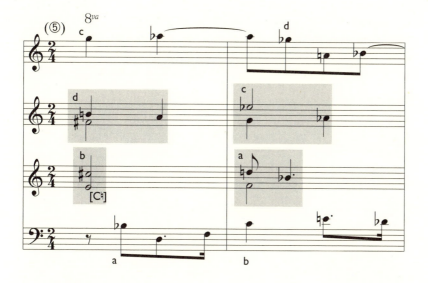

In Example 155, one bar after letter F, seven pitches occur with the first main beat of each measure—three in the
melody and four in the accompanying chord—giving a strong
accentuation to this vigorous statement of the previous light
scherzo theme. The end of the excerpt shows an ostinato using a, with fragmentary statements of b, c, and d.

Example 155a

Example 155b

Example 155b (continued)

Example 156 shows a passage that reaches a high level of chromatic density to intensify the final statement of the passacaglia theme shown earlier in Example 146. At this point the theme is in permutation ⑩ of the Matrix. The top voice of the harmonic setting is a full statement of this permutation. The other three voices are also formed from the trichords of the Matrix. Each half-note chord (strings) uses four pitches. The eighth-note figures in the upper voices (winds) use the eight remaining pitches over each chord. This means that all twelve pitches are heard in each $\frac{2}{4}$ bar.

The passage is shown in condensed form, and an excerpt from the full score (bars 2–6) shows the instrumental disposition. The main line is played by Violin 1, doubled in octaves by four horns and two bassoons. This brings out the theme clearly from the thick texture of the divisi strings in medium low register. The contrary pitches, which occur in seven high woodwinds with piano doubling, are placed well above the strings and horns. They participate in the overtone region without obscuring the fundamental harmony, which in itself contains no sharp dissonances.

Example 156a

Example 156b

Example 156b (continued)

Example 156c

Examples 157 and 158 will illustrate will illustrate the use of the previously shown chromatic techniques in larger formal contexts.

Example 157 is the first theme exposition of a clarinet and piano sonata. The clarinet part in the score sounds as written.

In this example, the style is adapted to the instruments; the piano part is more chordal than linear. In a number of instances, a single trichord is used vertically as a chord. An idiosyncrasy of this particular Tone-set is that certain permutations produce harmonious trichords, especially ⑥, which consists of major and minor triads. These are used when they occur, and when two are combined, they produce some of the effect of polytonality, though, of course, the total context is too chromatic to be simple polytonality.

The portion of the piece shown here happens to use all of the permutations from ① to ⑩, though the latter is incomplete.

Example 157a

Example 157b

Example 157b (continued)

Example 157c

Example 157c (continued)

Example 157c (Continued)

Example 158 is the entire first movement of a string quartet. The style is polyphonic throughout, with the thematic material shared by all four instruments.

There are three different Tone-sets for the three themes. Each set is marked by a Roman number, and the pitch on which it is based is shown in a box.

The character of the first trichord in each Tone-set is varied, the first being pentatonic, the second diatonic minor, and the third diatonic major. These choices are meant to support the idea of a strong, assertive first theme, a softer, more pliable second theme, and a bright energetic third theme (coda).

Tone-sets I and II are originally given with *B* as the first pitch. In use, however, they are not the same, in that II has a melody which chooses the second note of the trichord (*C♯*) for its beginning. This circumstance points out the fallacy of regarding the first note of a Tone-set as having special value similar to the first note of a tonal scale. The capital letters in boxes do not give a "key plan" for the work; they only give some information about the pitch levels. If, for example, I is on *E,* and then is on *A,* the level of theme will drop a fifth or rise a fourth (see p. 225, Tempo I, after the double bar). These are not changes of "key," but only changes of pitch-level, which may have something of the same effect as key changes in building a larger form.

Here are the various levels assumed by the three Tone-sets in this movement:

> Tone-set I—*B, E, A, G* (inverted), *B.*
> Tone-set II—*B, D, B♭, E♭* (inverted), *C♯, F.*
> Tone-set III—*G, G♯, C, E, D.*

These pitch-level changes may coincide with larger segments of the form, or they may occur at small divisions of a larger section. Both kinds of pitch-level change occur within this movement.

Usually, motives are identified with the Tone-set within which they originally occur, but this movement has a passage in which the head-motive identified with Tone-set I is developed within a section controlled by Tone-set III (see letter ⬛I). Such a possibility results, of course, from treating rhythm, not pitch, as the most distinctive and recognizable motivic element.

In the score example which follows, every Tone-set, pitch-level, order of permutation, and trichord is indicated from the beginning of the movement up to letter ⬛A. After that, individual trichords are not marked. They can be found easily enough by referring to the proper Matrix, transposing them when necessary.

Remember in counting tones, that some may be omitted in the *Cv* or other voices.

Example 158a

Example 158b

Example 158c

Example 158d

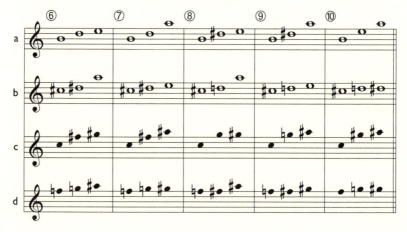

Example 158e

Example 158f

Example 158g

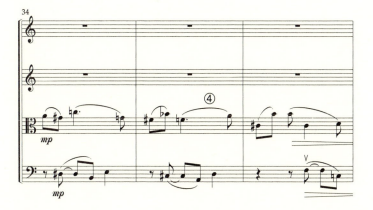

Some Special Cases

THE METHOD SHOWN IN THE EXAMPLES ABOVE, which involves a controlled pattern of trichord rotation, has as its basis a more generalized principle: in any twelve-note group, hexachords which succeed each other, or are combined in vertical placement, must be mutually exclusive. In other words, one six-note segment of the group must be the complement of the other.

The above principle can be applied to solve many compositional problems other than those shown here or in orthodox serial composition. The examples that follow illustrate a few situations in which the principle of this complementary relationship is applied *ad hoc*.

One of these situations is that in which diatonic material is incorporated within a chromatic structure. In Examples 159 and 160, chorale melodies are used within a chromatic setting.

In the chorale, *Mit Fried' und Freud' ich fahr dahin* (Example 159a), each phrase has a certain pitch content, varying from three tones (Phrase 2) to seven tones (Phrase 3). The chromatic complement consists of the tones not used, varying from nine tones (Phrase 2) to five tones (Phrase 3). The chorale melody is shown below, with a chart setting out the chromatic material (Example 159b). Also, the chromatic setting of the chorale and the beginning of the first variation are given.

242

Example 159a

Example 159b

Example 159c

Variations on "Mit Fried und Freud ich fahr dahin"

Example 159c (continued)

Example 160a shows two phrases of the chorale, *Heut' triumphieret Gottes Sohn*. In Phrase 1, the melody uses five pitches, leaving a complement of seven. In Phrase 2, the melody uses six pitches, leaving a complement of six.

In Phrases 1 and 2, the seven complementary pitches are divided into two conjunct groups of four, indicated by upwards and downwards stems with beams (a and b). In Phrase 3, the six complementary pitches are divided into two disjunct groups of three, again indicated by stems and beams.

The textural and rhythmical elements (unlike as in Example 157) are treated in "Bach" style. The chorale melody is in the tenor (middle staff). Contrapuntal parts lie above and below the melody, using the complementary pitches. Group a is placed above Group b, and Group b above Group a. The differentiation of the pitches and rhythms, and the registral distribution, all contribute to the independence of the individual parts and the clarity of the polyphony.

Example 160a

Example 160b

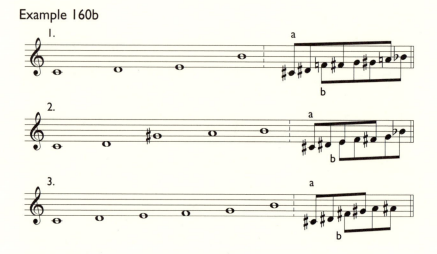

Example 160c

Heut' triumphieret Gottes Sohn (Chorale in tenor)

Example 160c (continued)

The basis of the piano variations in Example 161 is a block of notes made from three statements of a Tone-set in which Hexachord 1 contains the first six pitches of the chromatic scale, *G–C*, and Hexachord 2 has the other half of the scale, *D♭–F♯*. The order of the pitches is changed on each of the three statements (Example 161a).

The pitches of Hexachords 1 and 2 are placed together contrapuntally so that every interval formed is a dissonance. These must be either the tritone, the minor second (minor ninth), or the major seventh. Contrary motion is observed strictly (Example 161b).

The "block" is treated chordally, or with the tones dispersed. Example 161c shows the block itself, the theme, and the beginning of the first variation.

Example 161a

Example 161b

Example 161c

Variations for Piano

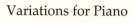

Example 161c (continued)

Example 162 is an excerpt from a setting of a translation of an anonymous baroque text used in a cantata by Carissimi for soprano and continuo. This setting is for the same medium (soprano and harpsichord with cello or gamba).

The technique is one which resembles baroque practice, in that the outer voices are controlled while the inner voices (the "realization") are free. The Tone-set is controlled only at the hexachordal level; the order is free within the hexachord. There are occasional free neighboring tones that lie a half-step away from the main tones.

Example 162a

Example 162b

Lament of Mary Stuart

Example 162b (continued)

Notes and Bibliography

Notes

CHAPTER 1. DERIVATION OF THE TONES

1. "When numbers assume form, they realize themselves in musical sound." Shih-chi, 1st. century B.C., quoted in the article on Chinese music by Bell M. Yung in *The New Grove,* vol. 4, pp. 260–262.

2. For example, see the history of the newly discovered universal laws governing processes and forms previously described as "chaotic," in the popular account by James Gleick, *Chaos: Making a New Science* (1987).

3. This date is suggested not from surviving documents, but inferred from the discovery of a set of twelve correctly tuned chimes dating from the Second Millennium B.C. Yung in *Grove.*

4. This legend is recounted in Chapter VII of *Enchiridion Harmonices* (Manual on Harmonics) by Nichomachus, a late Greek writer who was born in Gerasa (now Gerash, in Jordan) and who flourished around 100 A.D. There is a French translation by Charles Emile Ruelle, in *Collection des auteurs grecs relatif a la musique* (1881).

5. A description of the medieval monochord is given in *Enchiridion musices,* also called *Dialogus de musica* (ca. 920–924), once attributed to Odo of Cluny. An English translation is in Strunk, pp. 105–106. The method of calculation—using only the proportions of perfect consonances—is Pythagorean.

6. The earliest Chinese document giving a complete account of the derivation of the twelve tones used a method similar to this one. The first step in dividing the whole string is described as *san-fen sun-i* ("divide into three, take away one"), which gives the fifth. For the fourth, the string is divided into four, and one part is taken away. The result of this method is "Pythagorean." (Yung in *Grove*).

7. Distortions of these intervals occur in the tuning of some non-Western cultures so that the fifths and fourths are not in the proportions derived on the monochord, but are "tempered" to divide the octave into equal parts. As we shall see later, Western theory makes its own practical changes of the natural proportions when it arrives at a division of the octave into twelve equal parts.

8. In his treatise, *Epistola de ignoto cantu* (ca. 1030). In Strunk, 124.

9. *Musica Hermanni Contracti,* translated with introduction and commentary by Leonard Ellinwood (1936, reprinted 1952).

10. An excerpt of this treatise is in Strunk, pp. 219–227.

11. "Odo of Cluny," in Strunk, p. 106.

12. In *Craft,* I, pp. 48–49, Hindemith says the following about pentatonicism: "True, the pentatonic scale is a natural one ... it permits only a monotonous and inflexible harmony ... the melodies that are based on it are cool, undifferentiated, and remote."

Pentatonic patterns are used frequently by Hindemith in avoiding diatonic commonplaces, but chromaticism is also present, and only an occasional passage is purely pentatonic. Some works of Moussorgsky, Debussy, Ravel, Vaughan Williams and Bartok contain pentatonic passages, deriving from Eastern music or folk music of ancient origin.

13. In *Introduction to the Theory of Music* (1956), I attempted to offset the impression given by many definitions of chromatic that treat it as a coloration of the diatonic scale, or a mere filling-in of the whole-steps with half-steps. The relationship of pentatonic-diatonic-chromatic is discussed on pp. 101–103, and Chapter 12, pp. 142–153, is devoted entirely to a positive definition of chromaticism that does not treat it as a mere deviation from diatonicism.

CHAPTER 2. TUNING

1. "It is usual in geometrical construction to use such a phrase as 'Let this be a straight line'; but one must not be content with such language of assumption in the case of intervals. The geometrician makes no use of his faculty of sense-perception. . . . But for the student of musical science, accuracy of sense-perception is a fundamental requirement." *The Harmonics of Aristoxenus*, translated by H. S. Macran, 1902. In Strunk, p. 27.

2. Ptolemy (2d century A.D)
Claudii Ptolemæi, *Harmonicorum libri tres*. Latin translated by John Wallis (1699). Barbour, 16–21.

3. Reutlingen, Hugo de (Hugo Spechtsart ca. 1255–1359). *Flores musiciæ omnis Gregoriani* (1488). Barbour, 89.

4. Helmholtz, 446–451.

5. Ramis de Pareja, Bartolomeus (ca. 1440–1500).
Ramos, Bartolome. *Musica practica* (1482). Edited by Johannes Wolf (1901). Excerpt in Strunk, 200–204. Barbour, 89.

6. Aron, Pietro (1490–1545). *Toscanello in musica* (1523 and four later editions). Barbour, 26.

7. Zarlino, Gioseffo (1517–1590). *Dimonstrationi armoniche* (1571), p. 267. Barbour, 27–28.

8. The word is derived from the *gamma–ut* of Guidonian theory; but later meaning the whole range of notes.

9. Galileo, Vincenzo (1533–1592). *Dialogo della musica antica e della moderna* (1581). Barbour's reference (p. 57) is not included in Strunk, 302–322.

10. Vicentino, Nicola (1511–1572). *L'antica musica ridotta alla moderna prattica.* Barbour, 9, 144, 185.

11. Tsai-yü, Prince Chu (16th century). In Père Joseph Maria Amiot, *De la musique des Chinois* (Memoires concernant l'histoire, ... des Chinois), Vol. VI (1780). Barbour, 77–78.

12. Mersenne, Marin (1588–1648). *Harmonie universelle* (1636–1637). Barbour, 48, 79–87.

13. Lanfranco, Giovanni Maria (ca. 1490–1545). *Scintille de musica* (1533), p. 132. Barbour, 45.

14. *On the Sensations of Tone.* Chapters VIII and IX concern beats.

15. The phenomena of beats and difference tones described above in terms of wave interference have been shown to occur in the hearing process itself. They can result from non-linear response of a vibrating object under force. The ear's response is non-linear under pressure from loud sounds; difference tones are heard best under these conditions. Which parts of the ear act this way, and why, are still under investigation (see Backus, pp. 19–50).

16. Tartini, Giuseppe (1692–1770). *Trattato della musica* (1754). Wood, 29. Translated by Alejandro Planchart, JMT iv, 32.

17. Described in Barbour, 85.

18. Barbour, 87.

19. Quoted in Wood, 65.

20. Wood, 68–69.

21. Reproduced from Boatwright, 211.

22. Barbour, 89–91. See Note 5 above.

23. Barbour, 97–99.

24. Malcolm, Alexander (1687– 1763). *A Treatise of Music, Speculative, Practical and Historical* (1721, 1775, Reprinted 1969). Barbour, 3, 99ff, 143, 145.

———. Rousseau, Jean Jacques (1712–1778). *Dictionnaire de la musique* (1768). Barbour 100–101.

25. Hindemith, *Craft* I, 33–43.

26. Hindemith, *Craft* I, 34, 57.

27. Helmholtz, 428.

28. Helmholtz, 428.

29. Hindemith, *Craft* I, 155.

30. Barbour, 196–199.

CHAPTER 3. INTERVALS

1. The phrase is from the *Scholia enchiriadis* (now called "Scolica enchiriadis"), an early tenth century treatise from Northern France. "Disciple: What is a symphony [consonant interval]? Master: A sweet blending of certain sounds, ... " Strunk, p. 126.

2. See, for example, Charles Wuorinen's remarks on melodic construction in his *Simple Composition* (1979), p. 47ff.

3. Franco of Cologne's *Ars Cantus mensurabilis* is given in translation by Strunk; this excerpt occurs on pp. 152–153.

4. Helmholtz, 182–183.

5. *Senario.* Zarlino's term for the numbers 1–6. After the Partial Series was known (see p. 40), the term was applied to the Partials 1–6.

6. Detailed descriptions and diagrams may be found in Wood, 78–89; and Backus, 79–81.

7. Strunk, 113.

8. Strunk, 113.

9. In his treatise, *Micrologus,* Riemann-Haagh, p. 65: "Such a coming together of voices is done best with a whole-tone, ... but never with a minor third." In the convergence of a minor third to a unison in an ending, either the lower or the upper voice must move by a half-step, i. e., in modern terminology, an upper or lower leading tone.

10. Hindemith *Sonata for Violin and Piano* (1939) Copyright B. Schott's Söhne, Mainz, 1940.

Copyright renewed.

All Rights Reserved.

Used by permission of European American Music Distributor's Corporation, sole U.S. and Canadian agent for B. Schott's Söhne, Mainz.

11. Hindemith *When Lilacs Last in the Door-yard Bloom'd* Copyright, 1948, by Associated Music Publishers, Inc., New York.

Copyright assigned to B. Schott's Söhne, Mainz.

Copyright renewed.

All Rights Reserved.

Used by permission of European American Music Distributor's Corporation, sole U.S. and Canadian agent for B. Schott's Söhne, Mainz.

12. *Craft* III, 122.

13. Chapter 16 of *Craft* III, p. 90ff, contains descriptions of this sort of analysis. However, Hindemith uses nothing similar to the weighting system shown here.

CHAPTER 4. SONORITIES

1. The above is a short statement of Hindemith's view, expressed at the beginning of Section 9, Chapter III, *Craft* I.

2. In *Craft* I, Hindemith carries out the search for roots in all sonorities. The idea that the bass line takes over in more complex cases was a later view expressed in his teaching, 1945–48. Some late ideas concerning roots are found in *Craft* III, published posthumously in German, 1970.

3. "Thoughts on the Chordal Concept," *Essays on Music in Honor of Archibald Thompson Davison,* (Cambridge, Mass., 1957).

4. Such a classification is attempted by Hindemith in *Craft* I, which has a Table of Chord-Groups as a fold-out at the end of the volume. The broadest division is into A, *Chords without tritone*; and B, *Chords with Tritone*.

There are six categories—I, III, and V under A; and II, IV,

and VI under B. This chart has been criticized many times since it was published in English (1942). Hindemith did not rely on it at all in his teaching during 1945–1948; nor did he include anything like it in *Craft* III, although the principle of "fluctuation" remained intact.

In my early years of teaching at Yale (after 1948), I worked on a revision of this chart for use in teaching ear-training. When I attempted to go over it with Hindemith, his response was: "Since that time [when he wrote *Craft* I] I have come to hate charts!"

The symbols given here were developed during my classes at Yale after Hindemith left in 1953. The most important distinction between the categories used in these symbols and those defined by Hindemith is that chromaticism is recognized as one of the important ingredients—by its absence or presence.

5. This approach is different from Hindemith's, although it has the same basis. Hindemith's theory derives the roots of intervals from difference tones (with some inconsistency concerning the minor third). The roots of chords are then derived from the best interval in the chord. Here, the roots of chords, if they exist, are derived from a consideration of the whole spectrum of difference tones.

6. Hindemith's theory of tonal functions was never used by him to determine roots; he never made a direct connection between *tonic* and *root* as manifestations of the same thing: a psychological need for establishing hierarchical order.

CHAPTER 5. CHROMATIC MODES

1. There would appear to be some resemblance between the method of deriving the musical pitches by superimposing fifths and the principle of form-building in the fractal geometry of Mandelbrot, which is characterized by self-similarity in shape of all the parts, but a decrease (or increase) in scale (see Gleick, pp. 98–102).

One such construction is a Koch curve which uses a triangle as the basic shape. A smaller triangle is added to the
middle third of each face of the original triangle; then new
triangles are added to each of the new faces, and so on. There
is self-similarity in the shape of all the triangles, though in
ever-decreasing scale. The first step after the original triangle is the six-sided Star of David. As the form grows beyond that, it quickly begins to resemble a snowflake.

In the building of the tone-system by superimposing fifths,
the shape remains the same, but the pitches are higher and
higher in frequency. Higher frequency can be taken as
equivalent to smaller dimension or scale. This equivalency
corresponds to our experience with the vibrating string: all
other factors being equal (tension, weight, etc.), the longer
the string, the lower the pitch; the shorter the string, the
higher the pitch.

2. Pitch here is theoretical, not absolute. The notation chosen in the derivation of the tones (Chapter 1) begins with *F*,
not the usual *C*, because this brings in the seventh diatonic
note as *B*, and no accidental is required.

3. Fibonacci, Leonardo (also known as Leonardus
Pisanus). In his *Liber abaci* (1202) and *Practica geometria*
(1220), he introduced Arabic number notation into Europe.

4. There were other composers along with Schoenberg who
were experimenting with the idea of twelve-tone composition
in the decade before 1920. One whose work reached
crystallization in theory (if not in composed music)
was Joseph Mathias Hauer (1883–1959), whose "tropes"
(Zwölftontechnik: die Lehre von den Tropen, 1926) are somewhat similar to the "modes" proposed here.

Ten years later, Richard S. Hill (1901–1961) in his article,
"Tone-Rows and the Tonal System of the Future" (MQ XXII,
1936) discusses in specific detail Schoenberg's use of tone-
rows (up to that time), and suggests that twelve-tone composers should concentrate on the development of "functional

modes" which might endow the system "with an organized structure consistent with the requirements of the human mind." The article does not go beyond this interesting use of the work "mode" (instead of "trope") by offering theoretical or practical examples.

5. Berg, "Schliesse mir die Augen beiden mit den Lieben" (1925) from *Zwei Lieder.*

Text by Theodor Storm.

Copyright 1955 by Universal Edition A.G., Wien.

Copyright renewed.

All Rights Reserved.

Used by permission of European American Music Distributor's Corporation, sole U.S. and Canadian agent for Universal Edition A.G., Wien.

6. Along with a letter to Schoenberg (May 30, 1926) Berg included a memorandum on twelve-note composition which examines the possibilities of this row as part of his pre-compositional work on the *Lyric Suite.* He observes that it can be arranged in sequences of fifths or fourths, and that the tones 7–12 are at the interval of a tritone from the tones 6–1. Both features, of course, result from the derivation of the tones by superimposing fifths, as in Example 20. Berg also acknowledges the "discovery" of this row by Fritz Heinrich Klein (b. 1892), who employed it in his *Variations,* Opus 14, performed in Vienna in 1924 (*Berg-Schoenberg Correspondence, Selected Letters.* Edited by Julianne Brand, Christopher Hailey, and Donald Harris [1987], p. 348).

Berg *Lyric Suite*

Copyright 1927 by Universal Edition.

Copyright renewed.

All Rights Reserved.

Used by permission of European American Music Distributor's Corporation, sole U.S. and Canadian agent for Universal Edition.

7. Dallapiccola *Il Prigioniero.*
Copyright, Editioni Suvini Zerboni, Milano.
Used by permission.

8. The resemblance to "Es ist genug," however, was "coincidental," not planned (Berg-Schoenberg, letter of August 25, 1935, p. 446). After Berg had chosen to use four conjunct triads on the violin strings ("D major and similar violin keys were of course out of the question"), the remaining pitches (10, 11, 12) together with the 9th tone formed the whole-tone progression that begins the well-known chorale. Under the diagram of the row, little zeroes indicate the violin open strings, and on a separate staff with treble clef with the key signature of B major are the first four notes of the chorale: B–C♯–D♯–E♯.

PART TWO. PRACTICE

INTRODUCTION

1. This view was well-expressed by the turn-of-the-century theorist, Percy Goetschius (1853–1943): "Melody is the product of the source [chords], just as leaf, flower and fruit are the product of soil, root and branch." *The Homophonic Forms of Musical Composition* (1896, 1926), p. 12.

CHAPTER 6. TONE-SETS

1. One of Schoenberg's favorite students, who went from Vienna to Berlin with him in 1926. Zillig remained faithful to Schoenberg through the Hitler period. In 1955, Frau Schoenberg gave him the task of making the full score of *Jacobsleiter* (Stuckenschmidt, p. 246). Schoenberg's view was put forth in Zillig's *Variationen über neue Musik* (Munich, 1959), cited in Austin, p. 302.

CHAPTER 7. TWO-PART POLYPHONY

1. *Craft* I, Chapter V, Section 5, pp. 193–196.

CHAPTER 8. THREE-PART POLYPHONY

1. For an example, see the *Credo* by G. Legrant (ca. 1419), No. 56 in A.T. Davison and Willi Apel, *Historical Anthology of Music* (1949).
2. *Craft* I, Chapter IV, Section 3, pp. 115–121.

Bibliography

Aristoxenus. *The Harmonics of Aristoxenus,* translated by H. S. Macran (1902). Excerpt in Strunk, pp. 35–33.

Austin, William. *Music in the Twentieth Century from Debussy through Stravinsky* (1966).

Backus, John. *The Acoustical Foundations of Music* (1969).

Barbour, J. Murray. *Tuning and Temperament: A Historical Survey* (1953).

Boatwright, Howard. *Introduction to the Theory of Music* (1956).

Franco of Cologne. *Ars cantus mensurabilis* (ca. 1260). In Strunk, pp. 130–159.

Fux, Johann Joseph. *Gradus ad Parnassum* (1725); *Steps to Parnassus,* translated and edited by Alfred Mann (1943). Excerpt in Strunk, pp. 535–563.

Glarean [Glareanus], Heinrich. *Dodecachordon* (1547). Excerpt in Strunk, pp. 218–227.

Gleick, James. *Chaos: Making a New Science* (1987).

Guido d'Arezzo (d. ca. 1050).
———*Epistola de ignotu cantu* (ca. 1030). In Strunk, pp. 61–65.
———*Micrologus* (ca. 1025–1030). In Riemann-Haagh, pp. 61–65. In *Hucbald, Guido and John: Three Medieval Treatises,* translated by Warren Babb (1978).

Helmholtz, Hermann L. F. O*n the Sensations of Tone As a Physiological Basis for the Theory of Music,* translated and edited from the Fourth German Edition of 1877 with Notes and a new Appendix by Alexander J. Ellis (1885); New Introduction by Henry Margenau (1954).

Hindemith, Paul. *Unterweisung im Tonsatz.* 3 vols.

    I. *Theoretischer Teil* (1937).

    II. *Übungsbuch für den Zweistimmigen Satz* (1939).

    III. *Der Dreistimmigen Satz,* ed. Andres Briner, D. Meir and A. Rubelli (1970).

In English:

    ———. *The Craft of Musical Composition.*

    I. *Theoretical Part,* translated by Arthur Mendel (1942).

    II. *Exercises in Two-part Writing,* translated by Otto Ortmann (1942).

    III. *Three-part Writing*, translated by John Coleman (forthcoming).

(Page numbers given in the *Notes* refer to the English editions, except those for *Craft* III, which refer to the German edition.)

    ———. *Traditional Harmony,* (1943).

    ———. *Traditional Harmony II. Exercises for Advanced Students,* (1949).

    ———. Introduction to *Das Marienleben,* (1948).

    ———. *A Composer's World,* (1952).

Nichomachus (1st century A.D.). *Enchiridion harmonices.* French translation in Ruelle, Charles Emile, *Collection des auteurs grecs relatif a la musique* (1881).

"Odo of Cluny" (ca. 920–924). *Enchiridion musices* (also *Dialogus de musica*). In Strunk, pp. 103–116.

Rameau, Jean-Phillipe. *Traité de l'harmonie* (1722); *Treatise on Harmony* translated with an introduction and notes by Phillip Gosset (1971).

Riemann, Hugo. *History of Music Theory, Books I and II, Polyphonic Theory from the Ninth to the Sixteenth Century* (2nd edition, 1920), translated by Raymond H. Haagh, with preface, commentary and notes (1962).

Strunk, Oliver. *Source Readings in Music History*, Selected and Annotated by Oliver Strunk (1950).

Wood, Alexander. *The Physics of Music* (1944, Fifth Edition, 1950).

Yasser, Joseph. *A Theory of Evolving Tonality* (1932. Reprinted, 1975).

Zarlino, Gioseffo. *Le Istitutione harmoniche* (1588). Facsimile reproduction by Broude (1965). The two practical parts have been translated: Part III, *The Art of Counterpoint*, translated by Guy A Marco and Claude V. Palisca (1968); and Part IV, *On the Modes,* translated by Vered Cohen, edited with an introduction by Claude V. Palisca (1983).

Index

A

Aristotle 42
Aristoxenus 27, 257, 265
Arithmetic
  division 34–35
  mean 34
Arithmetical series 35
Aron, Pietro 31–32, 257
Atonal, Hindemith's view 50–51
Austin, William xvi, 263, 265

B

Bach, Johann Nicholaus 41
Bach, Johann Sebastian xiv, 41
Backus, John 258, 259, 265
Barbour, J. Murray xiii, 41, 257, 258, 259, 265
Bartok, Bela xv, xvi, 256
Basse fondamentale 83, 106. *See also* Rameau, Jean-Phillipe
Beats 38–39
  tuning by 39–40
Berg, Alban 118–119, 122–123, 262, 263
  compared with Webern 123
  letters to Schoenberg 262
  Lyric Suite 118, 126, 262
  "Schliess mir die Augen beide mit den Lieben" 118
  Violin Concerto 122, 126, 263
Blending Series 56–62

Boatwright, Howard 258, 265
  compositions
    A Song for St. Cecilia's Day (chorus and orchestra 140
    Choralbuch (organ) 241–247
    Five Songs (V. Hill) 189–191
    From joy to fire. Five Songs (Ursula Vaughan Williams) 188–189, 191–193
    Lament of Mary Stuart (soprano and harpsichord) 249–251
    Six Prayers of Kierkegaard (soprano and piano) 139, 194–197
    Sonata for Clarinet and Piano 138, 208–211
    String Quartet No. 2 137, 181–83, 202–203, 211–241
    Symphony (full orchestra) 184–187, 197–201, 204–207
    Three French Songs (high voice and piano) 194–195
    Variations for Piano 247–249
Brand, Julianne 262
Briner, Andres xii, 266

C

Cantus firmus (chromatic) 150–152
Cents, interval sizes in 29
Chant, Gregorian xiv
Chaos: Making a New Science (Gleik) 255
Chausson, Ernest 52
Chinese theory 4
  cosmological speculations 4
  equal temperament 256
  "Pythagorean" comma 26
  Shih-chi 255

Chord 82
    chord classification (Hindemith) 260
    general definition 82
Chroma, major and minor 46
Chromatic, chromaticism
    as shifting diatonicism 130
    chromatic density 193–197
    chromatic space 113
    definition of 14, 257
    formulas (symbols) 15–17
    full exploitation of 132
    groups 18–21
    in larger forms (examples) 208–241
    in the melodic minor scale 22
    modes 113–118
    restrictions on (Hindemith) 129
    scale 110
    spellings in chromatic music 159–160
    system, chart 110–114
    tonal and non-tonal 106
    treatment of intervals in 149–150
Ciliae, cochlea 67
Cohen, Vered 267
Combination tones 68. *See also* Difference tones
Comma
    Dydymian (syntonic) 27
    Pythagorean 26–28, 110
Complement, complementary tones 10, 241–247
Complementary voice 152–153
    examples 153–154
Concerto, Opus 24 (Webern) 123–125
Consonance-dissonance 58–60
Construction (monophonic, harmonic, polyphonic) 130–132
Contratenor 155

Cosmology, cosmological speculations
  Chinese 4
  Hindemith 48–49, 132
  Kepler 48–49
  Pythagorean 4
Counterpoint 174. *See also* Polyphonic, polyphony
Craft of Musical Composition, The. See Hindemith, Paul
Credo (Legrant) 264

D

Dallapiccola, Luigi 121–122, 142
Davison, Archibald Thompson 260
Debussy, Claude
  attitude towards dissonance 61
  pentatonicism in 256
  piano music of 9
Diabolus in musica 14. *See also* Tritone
Diatonic 10. *See also* Heptatonic
Didymus 27. *See also* Comma
Diesis, minor 46
Difference tones 39–40. *See also* Beats
  formed by intervals 62–64
Dimonstrationi armoniche (Zarlino) 257
Dissonances
  classification of 84
  dissonance level 157–159
  dissonant style, control of 170
Division (of a string), monochord 5–7
  arithmetic 34–35
  geometric 32, 33
Dodecachordon (Glareanus) 13, 265
Dominant
  function 74, 77–81, 98–105
  modal 74

E

Ear, structure of the 67–68
Electronic music, effect on composition 9
Ellis, C. H. 29
Enchiridion musices ("Odo of Cluny") 73, 256, 266
Epistola de ignoto cantu (Guido d'Arezzo) 256
Evolution of musical systems 4, 112–113

F

Fibonacci, Leonardo 112, 262
Fifth
  use in building a musical system 110
Fifths
  in supporting roots of sonorities 97
Fluctuation, harmonic (Hindemith) 130, 157
Fourier, J. B. 43
Frames, positive and negative 116, 117
Franco of Cologne 56–58, 72, 259, 265
Functional analysis (of sonorities) 96–105
Functional Series 81
Fux, J. J. x, 132, 265

G

Galilei, Vincenzo 36, 258
Gamut 36, 257
Geometric division, mean 32–33
Glarean [Glareanus], Heinrich 13, 265
Gleick, James 265
Goetschius, Percy 131
Gradus ad Parnassum (J. J. Fux) xii, 132

Greek theory
　Aristotle 42
　diatonic tones (gamut in medieval theory) 147
　modal names 12–13
　monochord 5
　Pythagoras 4. *See also* Pythagorean
Gropius, Manon 122
Grove, The New 255
Guido d'Arezzo 10, 28, 75, 257, 265

H

Haagh, Raymond 259
Hailey, Christopher 262–263
Harmonic Series. *See* Partial Series
Harmonices mundi (Kepler) 44
Harmonics, aural 68
Harmonie der Welt, Die (Hindemith) 49
Harmonie universelle (Mersenne) 38, 42
Harmonium, justly-tuned 49–51
Harris, Donald 263
Hauer, Joseph Matthia 262
Hearing and perception of intervals 66
　smoothness or roughness 67
　structure of the ear 67–68
Helmholtz, Herman L. F. xi, 29, 39, 40, 43, 257, 259, 266
　Just (natural) Intonation 49–50
　on beats 39, 258
　ranking of intervals 59
　tone quality analysis 43
Heptatonic (diatonic) modes 10–13
　authentic and plagal 12
　designated by numbers 13
　Greek and Latin names 12–13
　use in India and China 13

Hermannus Contractus 13, 256
Hexachords
  hexatonic modes 10
  in Tone-Sets 133
  positive and negative 114–118
Hindemith, Paul xii, xiii, xiv, xvi
  chord classification (chart) 260
  compositions by
    Harmonie der Welt, Die 49
    Requiem, "When lilacs last in the dooryard bloom'd" 77
    Sonata for Violin and Piano, 1939 76
  cosmology 48–49, 132
  derivation of the chromatic tones 47–48
  harmonic fluctuation 130
  harmonic fluctuation 157
  justly-tuned harmonium 51
  layered construction 131
  main functions of tonality 77
  pentatonicism 256
  restrictions on tritone and chromaticism 129–130
  root-progression 106
  roots of chords 260
  step-progession 150
  Switzerland xiii
  theoretical works
    A Composer's World xiv
    Craft of Musical Composition, The xi, xii, xiii, xiv, 132, 266
    Elementary Training for Musicians xii
    Exercises for Advanced Students xii, 266
    Introduction to *Das Marienleben* xiv, 266
    Traditional Harmony xii, xiv, 266
    Traditional Harmony II xii, 266

I

Instrumental music, influence on hearing and music 9
Intervals 4
   building musical systems from 109–110
   cosmological speculations about 3–5
   definition of 54
   derivation (monochord) 4–18, 148
   functional possibilities 78
   harmonic 56–62
   in non-Western cultures 256
   in the Partial Series 108–109
   interval relationships 74
   melodic 54–55
   proportions of 109
   ranking of harmonic intervals 72
   scale of values (weighting) 78–79
   treatment in chromatic music 149–150
Intonation. *See* tuning
Introduction to the Theory of Music (Boatwright) 257, 265
Istitutione harmoniche L' (Zarlino) xi, 267
   III. The Art of Counterpoint (Marco and Palisca) 267
   IV. On the Modes (Vered Cohen) 267

J

Just intonation 29–30, 30

K

Kepler, Johannes 44, 48–49, 132
   Pythagorean 48
Klein, Fritz Heinrich 262
Kolisch, Rudolph xvi

L

Lanfranco, Giovanni Maria 39, 258
Leading tones 75–77, 106
Lyric Suite (Berg) 118, 126, 262

M

Machaut, Guillaume xiv
Macran, H.S. 257, 265
Mahler, Alma 122
Main functions (of tonality)
  dominant 75
  leading tones 75–77
  polarity 77
  subdominant 75
  tonic 75
Malcolm, Alexander 46
Mandelbrot, Benoit 261
Marco, Guy A. 267
Mathematics, relation to music 3
Matrix 134–136
  utilization in melodic construction 136–140
Mean
  arithmetic 34–35
  chart 34
  geometric 32–33
Meantone tuning 31–35, 36
Meier, D. Daniel xii, 266
Melodic construction (from a Matrix) 136–140
Mersenne, Marin 38–42, 44, 258
Micrologus (Guido d'Arezzo) 259, 265
Miller, D. C. 43

Mode
  chromatic 114–118
  definition of 8
  Gregorian and Renaissance 12–13
  heptatonic (diatonic) 10–13
  hexatonic 10
  pentatonic 8
  Monochord
    derivation of intervals on 4–15
    Greek and medieval, description of 4–5
    use in tunings, 27, 28, 29, 30, 33, 35, 38, 41, 42, 44, 46, 47, 48
Monophonic construction 130
Moussorgsky, Modeste 256
Mozart, Wolfgang Amadeus 9
Music, aspects of 3
Musical construction, ways of 130–132

N

Neidhardt, Johann George 41
Nichomachus 255, 266

O

Occursus 75
"Odo of Cluny" 28, 73, 256, 266
Ohm, G. S. 43
Overtones 40, 108. *See also* Partials

P

Palisca, Claude V. 267
Partials, Partial Series
  as a basis for harmonic theory 108–109
  blending, in intervals 58–59, 68
  causing beats 40
  chords and scales in 108–109
  history and chart 42–44

Pentatonic, pentatonicism
  definition of 8
  Hindemith on 256
  scales 8
  sonorities (chords) 89
  trichords 142–146
  use by composers 256
  use in world music 8
Perception (of intervals) 66. *See also* Hearing
Phonodeik (Miller) 43
Piston, Walter 83
Poème (Chausson) 52
Polyphonic construction 130–131
Polyphonic, polyphony
  chromatic 148
  consonant-chromatic 170
  dissonant-chromatic 170–173
  early polyphony 147–148
  four-part 164–169
  "rules" of 148
  three-part 155–163
  two-part 147–154
  with more or less note-against-note 174–178
Porter, Quincy xiii
Prigioniero, Il (Dallapiccola) 121–122, 142
Proportions of intervals 109
Ptolemy 27, 29, 257
Pythagoras 4
Pythagorean and Neo-Pythagorean theory
  comma 26–28, 110
  cosmological speculations 4
  Hindemith 48–49, 132
  Kepler 48, 132
  medieval 256
  musical intervals and numerical proportions 4
  tuning 25–29

Q

Quintet, C Major, Opus 163 (Schubert) 76

R

Rameau, Jean-Phillipe xi, xiv, 82–83, 105–106, 266
Ramis de Pareja, Bartolomeus 29–30, 257
Ratios, of intervals 59
Ravel, Maurice 256
Requiem, "When lilacs last in the dooryard bloom'd 77
Reutlingen, Hugo de 29, 257
Riemann, Hugo 259, 265, 266
Roots
    of chords (Hindemith) 260, 261
    of chords (Rameau) 82–83
    of intervals 64–66
    of sonorities 93–96
    root-progression (Hindemith) 106
Rousseau, Jean Jacques 46, 259
Rubelli, Alfred xiii
Ruelle, Charles Emille 255

S

Sauveur, Joseph xi
"Schliess mir die Augen beiden mit den Lieben" (Berg) 118
Schoenberg, Arnold xiv, xvi. *See also* Zillig
    attitude towards dissonance 61
    diatonic music as a special case of twelve-tone music 141
    letter to Kolisch xvi
    letters from Berg 262
    row as theme 123
    Wind Quintet 119

Scholia (Scolica) enchiriadis 259
Schubert, Franz
  Quintet, C Major, Opus 163 76
Senario 61, 64–66, 71, 259
Series
  Blending 56
  Functional 81
  Partial 58
  Spatial 55
Shih-chi 255
Sol–fa (British) 49–50
Sonata for Violin and Piano, 1939 (Hindemith) 76
Sonority, sonorities
  building of 105–107
  control of 132
  definition of 83
  functional analysis of 96–105
  particular importance in Western Music 105
  roots of 93–96
Spatial Series 55–56
Spelling, in chromatic music 159–160
Step-progression (Hindemith) 150
Stravinsky, Igor xiv, xvi
Strunk, Oliver 256, 257, 258, 259, 265, 266, 267
Stuckenschmidt, H.H. 263
Subdominant 75–81
Subjective tones 68
Summation tones 68–72
Symbols (for sonorities) 84–86
Syntonic (Didymian) comma 27–28, 30

T

Tartini, Giuseppe 40, 258
Temperament, equal 37
    fretted instruments 36–37
    in non-Western cultures 256
    keyboard instruments 37–38
    nineteen-tone temperament (Yasser) 112–114
    thirty-one tone temperament (Vicentino) 113
Terzi suoni (Tartini) 40. *See also* Difference tones
Tièrce de Picardie 65
Timbre 42
Tonal space 54–55
Tonality 73–81
    dominant and subdominant 75
    hierarchical order 73
    leading tones 76–77
    main functions 77
Tone quality 42
Tone-set
    analysis of 145–146
    definition 133
    generation from trichords 141–145
Trichords (in Tone-sets)
    ancestry of 141
    permutations of 134–136
Tritone
    impact on the diatonic system 13–14
    occurence in the heptatonic scale 10
    restrictions on (Hindemith) 129
    use of b♭ to correct 14
Trumpet, natural 109

Tsai-yü, Prince Chu 38, 258
Tuning
    Helmholtz on 49–50
    Hindemith on 50–51
Tuning (intonation)
    equal 36–38
    fretted instruments 36–37
    Ideal Chromatic (chart) 47
    Just (natural) 29–30
    Just intonation as an ideal 44–47
    Meantone 31–35, 36
    Pythagorean 25, 28–29
    untempered: tolerance and adjustments 51–53

U

Unterweisung im Tonsatz. See Hindemith

V

Vaughan Williams, Ralph 256
Vicentino, Nicolo 37, 113
Violin Concerto (Berg) 122–123, 126

W

Wagner, Richard xiv, 130
Wallis, John 257
Webern, Anton von 123–126
    Concerto, Opus 24 123
Willaert, Adrian xiv
Wind Quintet (Schoenberg) 119–121
"Wolf" intervals 32, 36, 38, 113
Wood, Alexander 43, 258, 259, 267
Wuorinen, Charles 259

Y

Yale University xii, xiii
Yasser, Joseph xiii, 112–114, 267
Yung, Bell M. 255–256

Z

Zarlino, Gioseffo xi, xiv, 32, 257, 259, 267
Zillig, Winfried 141, 263

HOWARD BOATWRIGHT began his musical career as a solo violinist, making his debut in Town Hall, N. Y. in 1942. His first academic appointment was at the University of Texas (Austin) in 1943. In 1945, he went to Yale to study music theory and composition with Paul Hindemith, and joined the Yale faculty in 1948. There he taught music theory, conducted the University Orchestra, and served as concertmaster of the New Haven Symphony.

Boatwright's first book, *Introduction to the Theory of Music* (Norton) appeared in 1956. During a Fulbright to India, he wrote *A Handbook on Staff Notation for Indian Music* (Bombay, 1960), and several monographs on Indian music. Upon his return to Yale, he completed his edition of the larger prose writings of Charles Ives, *Essays Before a Sonata and Other Writings* (Norton, 1962). In 1964, Boatwright left Yale to become Dean of the School of Music at Syracuse University. In 1972, after a Fulbright to Romania, he resumed teaching at Syracuse until his retirement in 1983.

Musical composition assumed an important place in Boatwright's creative activities after his studies at Yale with Hindemith. His list of compositions now includes more than 80 titles, principally published by E. C. Schirmer and Oxford University Press up to 1979, and after that by Walnut Grove Press.

∾

C HROMATICISM THEORY AND PRACTICE was designed by David Ross using a Macintosh Quadra 800. The text was produced in Microsoft WORD 5.1a and the pages were set in Aldus PAGEMAKER 5.0.

The musical examples were produced in Coda Music Software's FINALE, converted to EPS files, translated into Adobe ILLUSTRATOR format using ART MUSIC from Two Bits Worth Software, and edited in Adobe ILLUSTRATOR 3.2.

The text is set in New Century Schoolbook. Gill Sans is used for captions. Additional fonts include Adobe Minion, TempiFont and MetricFont from Really Loud Fonts, Metronome and MetTimes from DVM Publications, Susato from ergo sum computer GmbH, and Rehearsal from Musiktypes. The music font is Petrucci from Coda Music Software.